A TRUE PERSON OF NO RANK

AWAKENING BUDDHA'S DREAM
TO SAVE THE WORLD

Joseph Bobrow

PRAISE FOR
A TRUE PERSON OF NO RANK

What does spiritual practice have to do with social engagement? A lot, as Joe Bobrow discusses in this perceptive reflection on their interaction. How does a "person of no rank" help to transform traumatic suffering? Drawing on his own experience as both a Zen teacher and a psychotherapist, Joe explores the connection between realization and personalization, insight and embodiment. Given the social and ecological challenges that face us today, it is essential for us to understand their relationship.

> —David Loy, author of *Ecodharma: Buddhist Teachings for the Ecological Crisis*; *Nonduality*; *Lack and Transcendence*.

This book is a wake-up call, and more. It has so much in it that actually wakes you up. You can feel inner seas part, old skin shed, and a brightness that your being is hungry for. Aspects of Buddhism and mental-health disciplines co-nourish and activate each other. I felt my spine tingle from the first words and a sense of life kept opening. And more – this work is not just an appeal to the individual to save himself but for a joint effort to save the world and each other. We are in this together and the life that informs us can give us more than we imagine.

> —Michael Eigen, author of *The Psychoanalytic Mystic*; *The Challenge of Being Human*; *The Sensitive Self*; *Flames from the Unconscious*.

For many decades, and through several books, Joe Bobrow has been developing a "multilingual" approach to Zen practice, one that combines the essence of the Zen tradition as he received it from his teachers, with insights and experiences from the psychoanalysis he has trained in and practiced. In *A True Person of No Rank* he adds to this crucially important ongoing project the element of compassionate social action, "saving the world," telling stories about the healing work he has done with war veterans and others. In the troubled world we live in now, he writes, we must all become true persons, sufficiently wise and healed within to be really able to help. This is a thoughtful and inspiring book.

—Norman Fischer, poet, author, and Soto Zen Buddhist priest. Author of *When You Greet Me I Bow: Notes and Reflections from A Life In Zen*; and *Selected Poems 1980-2013*.

Joseph Borrow brings alive the Buddhist roots of engaged spirituality – becoming an agent of compassion – with originality and inspiration.

—Tara Brach, Author of *Trusting the Gold and Radical Acceptance*.

Joseph's voice is a call to action for personal, social, and planetary healing. Everything matters. Dive in and be inspired!

—Koshin Paley Ellison, Author of *Untangled: Walking the Eightfold Path to Clarity, Courage and Compassion*.

Bobrow's thoughtful synthesis of a life-time of spiritual, professional, and communal explorations challenges you to examine the narratives that can waylay a spiritual path. In particular, this book holds up a mirror for Zen teachers and long-time Zen practitioners to consider anew how they align with the Buddha's dream.

—Wendy Egyoku Roshi, Co-author of *The Book of Householder Koans: Waking Up in the Land of Attachments*.

Joe Bobrow brings his lifelong experience as a Zen teacher, psychoanalyst and social activist to clear up eons of psychological and spiritual confusion! Perennial questions about unity and differentiation, self and no-self, the role of the unconscious, individual vs. societal awakening – he takes them on fearlessly in this warm and knowledgeable book, filled with moving stories of transformation and love. I really enjoyed this book.

—Trudy Goodman, Founding Teacher, InsightLA

Joseph Bobrow's new book is a refreshing deep dive into the nature of "true self," reworking sometimes incomplete Western perspectives on *anatta* (no self) with a view that is both true to the original Buddhist teachings but also attuned to the fact that "The world is burning. People are destroying it." Roshi/psychoanalyst Bobrow describes a person of no rank who is able to embrace (not discard) a specific version of personhood and compassion in order to ease the suffering of others and defend our embattled world. Deep and suitably irreverent, existential and yet personal, this book is recommended to those wishing to look more deeply into the nature of consciousness and the implications of the dharma for a world on the precipice of very frightening things.

    —John Briere, PhD, Emeritus Professor of Psychiatry, University of Southern California School of Medicine, Co-editor of *Mindfulness-oriented interventions for trauma: Integrating contemplative practices* (Guilford).

In *A True Person of No Rank*, Joseph Bobrow explores the power of embodiment – building our capacity for love and sharing our compassion with the world. This book is a reminder of the sacredness of being alive and the importance of fully living the awakenings we experience.

    —Sharon Salzberg, author of *Lovingkindness and Real Change.*

To Tom Rosbrow, with appreciation

A True Person of No Rank
Awakening Buddha's Dream to Save the World
Joseph Bobrow

Published by
The Sumeru Press Inc.
PO Box 75, Manotick Main Post Office,
Manotick, ON, Canada K4M 1A2

Cover: Zen poet Han-shan and his comrade Shih-te.

"Han-shan epitomizes the peak-dweller and his poems shimmer with mountain light. Other of his poems swell with earthy feelings, not just compassion or delight, but also anger, longing, sourness, pride, loneliness, sorrow, worry. How could these not also be the feelings of an awakened mind?" – *The Roaring Stream*, Foster and Shoemaker (Eds),The Ecco Press, Hopewell, NJ, 1996, p. 54 (slightly compressed.)

ISBN 978-1-896559-85-8

LIBRARY AND ARCHIVES CANADA CATALOGUING IN PUBLICATION

Title: A true person of no rank : awakening Buddha's dream to save the world / Joseph Bobrow.
Names: Bobrow, Joseph, author.
Description: Includes bibliographical references.
Identifiers: Canadiana 20220233225 | ISBN 9781896559858 (softcover)
Subjects: LCSH: Buddhism and social problems. | LCSH: Community development—Religious aspects—Buddhism.
Classification: LCC HN40.B8 B63 2022 | DDC 294.3/376—dc23

For more information about The Sumeru Press
visit us at *sumeru-books.com*

CONTENTS

CONTENTS

There is a *true person of no rank*
who is constantly coming and going
from the portals of your face.
Who is that *true person of no rank*?
— Linji Yixuan, 9th-century Zen master

INTRODUCTION

The many beings are numberless;
I vow to save them.
Greed, hatred, and ignorance *rise endlessly*;
I vow to abandon them.
Dharma gates are countless;
I vow to wake to them.
Buddha's way is unsurpassed;
I vow to embody it fully.[1]

The world is burning. People are destroying it. Some are stoking the combustion by fanning the flames of hate-filled violence, amplifying and manipulating our deepest anxieties, preying on a set of deadly multidimensional crises, exploiting public shock and anguish for private gain. The most toxic and corrosive psychic fuels are intensified and spread like wildfires with purposely false information.

In classical Buddhism, *samsara*, the world of sorrow and pain, is sometimes associated with heat and fire. The heat of the blind passions. But today we are living in a massive emergent samsara where we are witnessing and participating in the destruction of our planet and its creatures and the degradation of the finest human qualities. It seems out of control, and at times, it is out of control. We suffer from helplessness, despair, terror, and numbness; the risk, perhaps the increasing likelihood, that the human species and thousands of others with it, will not survive.

In the Four Infinite Vows, cited above, Zen practitioners chant "Greed, hatred, and delusion rise endlessly." These are referred to as the Three Poisons. Although I've chanted them for fifty years, today I see more clearly than ever just how toxic the Three Poisons are, unbridled and sometimes masquerading as benevolence, reasonableness, or normality. The richest few have their fortunes balloon as the many struggle to survive. Hatred becomes normalized, with those in power "saying the quiet things out loud." The psychotic denial of objective reality, along with the cynical and deadly mind-manipulation and gas-lighting of tens of millions of us, is frighteningly real, if delusional. In the first line of the Four Infinite Vows, we chant, "Innumerable beings, I vow to save." Saving all beings is at the heart of Mahayana Buddhism. The boat is big, all can come on board as we row to the other shore.

I remember saying to Aitken Roshi early in my practice, "Saving, that has a messianic ring, almost like rescuing beings from original sin; saving their souls." He responded, "Then think 'protect.'" I could relate to that and let go of the messianic associations to the word 'save.' But today, 'save' is neither hyperbolic, messianic, or moralistic. It's up to all of us to turn the ship around. To save our planet, our fellow humans, and the more than human world. We must shepherd our finest qualities and share them vigorously. Aitken Roshi would sometimes say we are all practicing Buddha's dream, cultivating compassion and wisdom for the benefit of all beings. Now more than ever we need to cultivate and bring to bear all our capacities, counteract numbing and despair, and, individually and collectively, unleash wise and responsive action to save the world.

In this book, I take a fresh look at Buddha's vision for an awakened person and her awakened activity. I examine the true self (also referred to as no-self) that is at its heart, and unpack some misunderstandings that can hinder us on the path and impede the distinctive, empowered expression of our realization. I explore a true person of no rank, a Zen expression of no-self, and the notion of an agent of compassion. It takes an insubstantial person of substance, (not fixed or permanent but grounded) not only to survive these dire times but to actively participate in saving the planet and healing the world. It takes a differentiated *person*, an *agent* of compassion, to bring to bear the insights of oneness and radical interconnection at the heart of Buddha's dream.

"One must have a self before one loses it" is a notion that has gained popular currency. But I think the two are neither mutually exclusive nor simply sequential. Rather than having to construct a self *before* we can discover no-self, I think *it takes a (distinctive, personalized) agent to fully embody our essential (no-self) nature.* And as we unravel, experience, and realize the empty, multi-centered nature of all beings and of consciousness itself, the (particular, personalized) self and its unique qualities are potentiated – brought to life and fruition.

In *Zen and Psychotherapy,* I described how spiritual practice (represented by Zen) and emotional growth (represented by psychoanalysis) were "partners in liberation." In *A true person of no rank*, I build on this conversation and introduce a third interlocutor, social action, to form an emancipatory trio. These three have been interweaving in my life from early on. We can't really *bring* these dimensions – we can call them psyche, spirit, and world – together; they *are* together. They each bring their own perspectives to forge an integrative myth, an ancient dream updated, in which the individual and the collective arise and work in tandem. A story where meditation, insight, and benevolent action arise and operate in concert.

In this book, I explore how mindfulness and Buddhist practitioners embody and fail to embody their practice and insight in daily living. Today, when truth and reality themselves are up for sale, we must respond to the anguish of our world creatively. As I articulate and update a true person of no rank, I explore other guiding myths of awakened conduct, among them the Bodhisattva and the Arhat. I introduce the agent of compassion. Person, agent – each is in accord with true no-self. How can that be? Don't we "let it all go? Forever." I weave an original and enhanced, experience-near story of engaged living that recognizes and brings forth our full humanity for the benefit of all beings.

True self or no-self is not selflessness. It is not even something called "no-self." It is not on the register of self and non-self, selfish and selfless; therefore we *call* it 'true' or 'no-self' or 'the person of no-rank.' It is dynamic, full of idiomatic human qualities and capacities we must not waste by misrecognizing and discarding them. Open and at rest, it is responsive, like Avalokitesvara, the Bodhisattva of compassion, to the sounds of the world, the sounds of anguish. Like Manjusri, the Bodhisattva of wisdom, it comes forth wisely, personalized and in accord with circumstances. With unbridled greed, hatred and delusion running rampant, our world needs the vigor and diversity of our true selves, true persons of no-rank, agents of compassion, more than ever, just as the Jeweled Net of Indra, the ancient Buddhist image of intimacy and particularity, needs each jeweled point in the goddess Indra's limitless net to shine forth distinctively for the benefit of all.

Let's say (play) that true self or no-self is actually *whole self*: radically inclusive, unfettered, unhindered, and unimpeded in its responsiveness. Unsequestered, undivided, not isolated, fragmented, or permanent. It includes the bombs, the fires, the poison, the greed, hatred, and ignorance, the joy, the pain – all we can see and all we can't see, all of it. Everything 'outside' and 'inside,' conscious and unconscious. All belong. A limitless belonging.

Realizing and living this, however, requires an underlying *sense* of self, a sense of agency, a sense of personhood, a sense of worth and freedom and empowerment.

These are the backcloth, the foundational elements: when they're not there or when they're compromised, they obtrude and we suffer; when they are well-enough established and operating, we don't suffer [so much]. "True self," "no-self," and "whole self" are absent, invisible, making no claims.

Old master Yuan-Yu said, "When bodhisattvas who live a householder's life cultivate practices of home-leavers, it is like a lotus blooming in fire. It will always be hard to tame the will for fame and rank and power and position, not to mention all the starting points of vexation and turmoil associated with the burning house of worldly existence. The only way is for you to realize your fundamental, real, wondrous *wholeness* and reach the stage of great calm, stability and rest."[2]

PROLOGUE

Old Zen ancestor Linji raised the 'poor' person of no-rank and saddles him with the unenviable label 'true' to boot. Why dredge up an old concept from the scrap heap? Because we need this person now more than ever. In these dark and crazy times, when truth and reality are themselves up for sale, maleficence masquerades as helping, and unbridled greed, hatred, and delusion are rampant and commonplace, it's a radical act to draw a breath freely and exhale long and slow. It's revolutionary to stand up, sit down, laugh, and weep. Buddhist living is not exceptional; it expresses our full humanity. Being human is wondrous and shockingly ordinary. It hurts and delights; it's real. *Real* quickens, nourishes, and transforms.

Poor person of no rank, unholy, unfinished and done with becoming. Full of holes, he lets in sounds of the world and hears voices sorrowful and aching to blossom, belong and contribute. And he responds. As he transforms his own suffering he naturally recognizes and responds to other beings. We need him. His peace, his pieces richly composting, responsive to humans and other beings near and far. Body and mind unencumbered, heart and soul untethered, available.

Not striving for perfection or pushing away evil, her activity is naturally in alignment with shifting conditions. Unsanctimonious and benevolent, she learns from children, animals, and seniors, the annoying prophetic voice, and the subtle impacts of her own conduct. She walks the ancient Way, living Buddha's dream.

Story gets a bad rap these days. "It's just your story, see through your story, let go of your story." Why not eviscerate yourself from your perennial roots while you're at it! *Dream* too finds scant respect, relegated to nighttime or equated with a distracted drift. Yet,

It is dream that animates
what we create
in our wake

as we go about
our nights and days

we wake dream
bring it
to life

This book is Buddha's dream, but it's really Bobrow dreaming Buddha. For the author's enjoyment and the benefit of beings near and far. Blame Bobrow, not Buddha. This Bobrow fellow has poked around in Buddha fields and tasted nutriment and poison. In Zen, there is a sword that kills and a sword that gives life: Which sword do you want? Put aside loss and gain, dare to be uncertain, and welcome new ways of seeing and being.

1

TRUE NO-SELF

ORIGIN DREAM

After years of wandering, searching many paths, many teachers, after painful austerities and repeated dead-ends, Shakyamuni Buddha sat down under a pippala tree and resolved not to get up until he had penetrated the question that had animated him for years: Why is there such suffering? After long practice, one morning he opened his eyes at dawn and glimpsed the morning star. All conceptual formulation, all niggling doubts fell away and he exclaimed, "Now I see that all beings are Buddha-nature; it is only their attachments and delusions that keep them from bearing witness to this fact." In another telling he said, "All things and I have awakened together."

It was as if the Buddha had awoken from a dream-like fog. And yet, what he went on to teach presents our human existence itself as a dream, not a delusion, but something vast, ungraspable, impermanent, yet precious, transformative, and closer to us than our own noses.

After the Buddha's experience, he sat and savored it. Eventually though, moved by requests from former fellow seekers, he got up and responded, entering the social field to share his insight, to give and take with all, to awaken and heal.

WORDS

Zen is a transmission beyond name and form. What a tired old slogan! We use words and get used by them, for better and worse. With words we conceal and reveal, deceive and perceive. Silver-tongued Zen ancestor Zhaozhou challenges us, "Say something without moving lips or tongue." I accept the challenge, doomed from the start.

Some words are so saturated I won't touch them. Some have become atrophied – conventional wisdom – I'll challenge them. Don't worry if at first you don't get it; not-knowing is your ally. When you hear a word, say "compassion," watch how you react. "Yes, I know that." An unruly old teacher used to repeat loudly and incessantly, "Only don't know!" Listen to this true no-self story as if for the first time, and the as-if will drop away. You'll hear the words and the music afresh, as intended, just for you.

⟞⟞

How do you define yourself? In T'ang period China, title and rank offered cultural and personal structure, if oppressively at times. Old ancestor Linji pulled up the rug and flung the door wide open:

> There is a person of no rank who is constantly
> coming and going from the portals of your face.
> Who is the true person of no rank?

Linji invites us to live freely without cleaving to title or rank or any iden-tification at all. Without dualistic constriction: Enlightened or deluded; Buddha or ordinary person; success or failure; mind or heart; self-interest or collective interest. He also subverts fixed role-based identities. But don't think he means anything goes.

True no-self, the root of no-rank and no-title, is the most easily mis-understood Buddhist teaching. We formulate it ("no-self, nothingness, emptiness") and then react to it – our own formulation – with confu-sion, dread, and desire. Some want nothing more than to eliminate all trace of self, thoughts, feelings, and distinctiveness. *To be nobody.* Maybe then there will be less pain, more gain. Replace an ordinary persona with a Buddhist persona, and then walk around acting the part.

Nothing is not something called nothing.

Far from being literally void of stuff, our true no-self nature is dynam-ic, emergent, full of possibility, teeming with potential and unformed qualities.

A good no-self is a terrible thing to waste.

Far better than chucking mental and emotional content is to experience our true no self, "a true person of no rank" directly. The apparent paradox is that only by "forgetting" the self can we truly come to ourselves, come to *experience* the stuff of the self as the sacred. Self and object fall away. Yamada Roshi, (old teacher), had an awakening for the ages. At the time a middle-aged businessman and Zen student, he was returning from work in Tokyo one day. While reading on the train, he came upon the phrase: "Mind is none other than the mountains and rivers and the great wide earth, the sun, the moon and the stars." He had read the words many times before, but they had not come alive for him. Everything fell away, and there was only great laughter. What was so funny? Through an experience of empty infinity, we can know *directly* (in contrast to *knowing about*) the personal and the sacred as identical. For Yamada Roshi, this was less the kind of falling apart that we associate with fragmentation and dread than it was a *falling into fertility*.

He would always urge us to realize our essential (no-self) nature. But he also enticingly confused us by saying, "Zen is the perfection of character." Does awakening perfect character? Conduct? We'll dive into that morass later. Now I'll tweak his words to my own devices: Zen practice refines a true person of no rank. Baby needs the bathwater.

To practice Zen is not to eliminate or punish the self, to demonstrate how much privation we can take. It's letting go of self-preoccupation as we immerse in the task at hand, the particular circumstances of this moment. Let's chip away at notions of true no-self and see what emerges.

BOOGEYMEN

Many Buddhists are allergic to I, me, and mine. Positively aversive. Twisting themselves into pretzels of avoidance, while amplifying the ghostly entities they're grappling with. Some teachings encourage us to say, "There is anger," rather than, "I am angry." I know, I know, when we're stuck, this might help us "disidentify" and "create space" to observe, maybe. But imagine this: You get home from work and your honey conveys displeasure about something you did or didn't do. And you say, "Oh, *there was* anger." Might need a new set of dishes after the dust clears.

How about me and mine? Once I noticed a mother on the beach with her young child. The toddler began wailing after another child took her pail. The mother scolded the toddler, "Don't say mine; it's everybody's." This was 1970s Maui, with the Age of Aquarius mores of the era. But I cringed then as I cringe today recounting it, acutely aware of how timeless it is. To realize the inherent symbiosis among beings and share freely, it helps to have a well-established me and mine, supporting us as we let go and come forth.

Some encourage Buddhist practitioners to eschew the sense of self. This is quite appealing to those of us who have not built one that's hardy enough: I'm pretty good at being nobody; maybe my deficits will work in my favor.

When you jettison your sense of self, you think you're gaining an exemption from anguish, but you do so at your peril.

How about the king of boogeymen, ego? I'm partial toward mine; my ego capacities, that is. They're hard won; significant repair and construction went into them. These capacities – judgment, perception, memory, emotional regulation, among others – take regular maintenance and grow hardier with use.

Ego is not a problem, ego inflation is. So are ego impoverishment and ego aggrandizement, by which we compensate for the gaps in our development wreaked by overwhelming trauma. I'll simplify: "My stuff doesn't smell." Or, "What stuff?" "I've cleaned up my act." "Look how selfless I am." How self-centered we become in our self-denial, how self-righteous in our self-sacrifice.

> The congregation is gathered in an orthodox synagogue for the High Holy Days, and they are fervently *davening* [praying], rocking side to side. The religious climate is thick, alive with the devotional spirit. The rabbi is facing the Torah, chanting, praising the Almighty, "Lord, I am not worthy! In my heart I know that I am nothing." The cantor listens to the rabbi's words and joins him at the ark. He declares, "Lord, even though I have led your children today in fervent prayer, in beautiful sacred melody, I know that I am really nothing." Then a simple Jew who has been praying devotedly all day stands up in the middle of the synagogue and cries out, "Lord, I just want you to know I am nothing!" The cantor leans over to the rabbi and whispers, "Look who thinks he's nothing!"

It's easy to disavow affliction and painful emotion and embrace the idea of being nothing. It's more difficult to grow capacity by learning to stand (withstand), understand, and let go. "Letting go" has become a triviality: What do we let go of? An old teacher once said, "Non-attachment, all I hear is non-attachment! If you weren't attached, you'd be dead!" Sticky, that non-attachment, easy to get caught up in offshoring the troublesome "story" with its "ego" reigning supreme. Proceeding in this manner is a good recipe for cultivating impoverishment.

The occasional fleeting thought is of no consequence. It comes and goes. Even a thought bubble can dissolve when we recognize it. A range of feelings and moods rise and fall. There is always a condition, as my teacher, ancestor Dawn Cloud Aitken, told us. He invited us not to struggle for a perfect state. But we're drawn to Zen by its reputation as the clearest of clear paths, nothing messy to intrude! Ironic, don't you think, that great ancestors like Dogen tried so persistently to disabuse us of such notions,

> Though clear waters range to the vast blue autumn sky
> How can they compare with the hazy moon on a spring night?
> Most people want to have it pure white,
> But sweep as you will, you cannot empty the mind.[3]

There are self-generated obstacles alright: Fixed, habitual, even addictive versions of self and versions of self with others. Selective storylines that exert such a pull that it seems well-nigh impossible to spring free and immerse oneself in this inhale or in going shopping. These and the draw they exert are attachments – they don't refer to needing food, shelter, safety, friends, and so on. Or the motivating aspiration to awaken, be free from anguish, to use myself well. Or a narrative fueled by the desire that all beings realize themselves and flourish.

⤙⤚

"Just sit with it," many teachers used to instruct; when letting go gets gnarly, the gnarly get going. They took as given what is not a given: the capacity to stand affliction. It's painful to face fixed, emotionally charged, repetitive storylines that exert such a grip, not to mention unhitch from them. We've ingeniously constructed them to keep traumatic experience at bay, so we're seriously invested: Can't live with them, can't live without them. True divestment takes time and practice.

When a particularly sticky thread has you in its grip, watch it carefully, observe the subtle interplay of thought, feeling, sensation and mental reaction as it generates and maintains anguish. As the thread untangles and you're no longer in the grips of a repetitive afflictive loop, when you have available awareness to invest, return and invest it here and now. The tangles of the "mind" are endless; you can spend a lifetime trying unsuccessfully to comb them out once and for all.

We also hold hidden requirements: this is how it is, but that's how it's *supposed* to be. Deliverance beckons, if only... [fill in the blank]. We cleave to fixed versions of self and of self with other beings while searching for liberation. Curiously they make us feel more secure. These requirements, along with insufficient capacity to withstand pain, obscure and imprison us. We chase out through the five senses, restlessly searching for relief. This is *tanha*, and it breeds more *dukkha*. With dedicated attentiveness, unhitch from reliance on words and mental formations, letting the garden variety kind pass and unraveling the sticky, fixed and repetitive ones. This is part of working with attachment. Take note: Zen is not Mr. Clean: good for tables, counters, windows, floors, and bathtubs. Awakening doesn't grant an exemption from emotional pain that may need attention in other healing settings.

See why it's so appealing to offload the whole kit and caboodle?

Just as we can (incorrectly) imagine no-self as a vacuum, so can we imagine in a rather concrete way the whole self as a cabinet full of stuff, all kinds of elements, brought together, hanging in balance. Rather, when it feels together, when we're not turning away, when there is a robust enough sense of self, personhood, and agency, then capacities are growing to withstand, tolerate and learn from our experience, especially when it's afflictive. We may even realize that the feelings, thoughts, sensations that are so difficult to face, that we push away or get tangled up in, are themselves expressions of awakening. Samsara itself is Nirvana. When these capacities are operating well-enough, the self, the person, and the agent are absent; invisible supports that facilitate letting go of needing to be self-obsessed. No-self, true self and whole self are simply irrelevant and not in play.

Why this splitting hairs? Who cares? And why does it matter? I've seen scores of people, many experienced Zen practitioners, who still harbor the idea that the purpose of zazen is to stop thoughts, and that the painful ones in particular can be suppressed or eliminated. The result is a flattening out of liveliness, a loss of energy, a stiff, zombie manner and practice; all personal contents, and qualities, flushed out of the system. This can paralyze and tie us up in knots. A sense of distinctive Dharma expression and the activity of personalizing our practice often don't materialize, or are dry, truncated and impoverished. Agency, voice, empowerment, vigorous expression and responsiveness, are impaired.

I recall a meeting with a Zen student where what unfolded finally was his shame at feeling proud about something. Maybe he'd got a job he had worked toward. He realized that he'd been unaware of judging this as self-centered and realized that this had been jamming up his practice and his life. Someone who feels elated at finding a nice place to live after a long search has a good enough sense of self to be able to let loose with glee. This is the obverse of being self-aggrandizing, self-absorbed and self-inflated. Likewise with sorrow. Is self a *klesha* here? A toxin? A defilement?

I recall going to dokusan with Maezumi Roshi after my father died in 1977. I entered the room and said, "I'm Joe and I'm feeling sad; my father just died." Roshi replied, "When your father dies and you feel sad, that's sad Buddha." How liberating! In 1983, Thich Nhat Hanh walked from his stone cabin along the stream into the old Tassajara Zen Mountain Monastery dining room which was packed to the rafters with earnest priests and laypeople, sitting with their best posture, albeit a bit stiffly. Thay arrived and sat silently, with a half-smile. After a while he said softly, "Does the silence bother you?" People shuffled around to be or at least appear more at ease. "Please," he said, "Enjoy your breathing." There was a collective sigh. Ahh, many tight chest muscles loosened; enjoying the body and the breath wasn't indulgent. If we've offloaded our humanity and important capacities, how can we embody our experience of awakening with all beings? Yamada Roshi arrived at the Maui Zendo in 1972. In the depth of *sesshin*, prior to *teisho*, we could hear him coming at fifty paces, clanking down the long wooden hallway in his wooden *zories*, the strong whiff of after shave lotion preceding him. Was he acting like a special case, self-inflated, breaking our rules about walking silently and not using perfumes? I found him 'Bien dans sa beau.' At ease. The Dalai Lama and Ven. Thich Nhat Hanh are often asked if they ever get angry. As true *persons*, they always respond that they do. It's how they construe and respond that's key.

So, returning to our question, Who cares? We should. In today's world, we need all hands on deck; energized, vital, responsive. It's relevant because models, say of no-self and emptiness, inform. Even in Zen where they are generally considered conceptual formations and eschewed, they still exist and inform. Ideals and myths and dreams are fluid like true no self, yet this does not prevent them from powerfully informing our conduct, being and impacts.

Self has many faces: When is it a klesha? An obstruction, a defilement? We know self can tyrannize, ourselves and others. Torturous, ruminating or nursing resentment, an arrogant or entitled kind of self-activity afflicts. And collectively, consider ideology, how it conceals malign motives revolving around rank, as in power and control; simple self-aggrandizement, with no concern for the other.

Yet, self-experience can be benevolent, expansive, connecting; it can build capacities for the journey ahead. Feeling happy, encouraged, gratified at how a common project has gone, for example; is this 'self-referential?' We need to tease this out, to assure that ours is a sustainable, human myth. More on this in the next two chapters, where we examine a wild card we do well to take seriously: the unconscious.

I hope that the way I am using (some might say misusing) a true person of no rank illuminates how the personal and impersonal, the particular and the universal, and maybe the emotional and the spiritual intersect, and how this intrinsic interplay makes possible ongoing personal character development *and* being-of-service in the world, without the usual inherent conflict.

THE OLD WORTHIES WEIGH IN

The old worthies had something to say about persons and personalizing,

> Even if, in order to make progress, you sorted out all the Chan teachings…your mistake would still consist in searching for proclamations from other people's tongues. So how should one approach what has been transmitted? There must be a real *person* in here! Don't rely on some master's pretentious statements or hand-me-down phrases that you pass off everywhere as your own understanding. (Yunmen, p 85)[4]

I'm not talking about persona. Yunmen says,

If you want to live freely or die, go or stay, to take off or put on your clothes, then right now recognize the person who is listening to my words. He is without form, without characteristics, without root, without source, and without dwelling place, yet he is brisk and lively. (p. 41)[5]

Brisk and lively, and accessing and freely sharing unselfconsciously all his distinctive qualities. Having sloughed off self-preoccupation, sprung free from self-absorption, this person also laughs and weeps, sings and dances, has access to the entire repertoire of talents, inclinations and distinctive qualities of what some might disparagingly call self.

Yamada Koun Roshi, one of my teachers, captures the joy, vigor and play of no self dreaming, a true person of no rank, the insubstantial person of substance,

Now I will say my last words. The last word, you know, that is a *koan*. I will say the last word, ha! Earlier, Joe pointed to that picture over there, and asked if I knew that person [a picture of a younger Yamada Roshi in robes, holding the flower he was given as he stepped off the plane in Maui for the first time]. I asked him, "Do you know him?" Joe replied, "I do not know him." I too said that I didn't know him at all. I am afraid to have to tell you that what I have said this evening has been deceiving, that I have deceived all of you [laughter]. And I must say that I have deceived myself too [more laughter]. But you know [pointing to his own head], I like him [even more laughter]. And we need him, we cannot do without him. This afternoon at Iao Park, I was reading a poem of William Merwin's in a book he gave to me. This! – is it the words I say, or is it the poem of William's? I do not know. It is like a dream. That is all. Sayonara. It is time to go to bed.

SELF AS KLESHA

One day while driving I happened on a radio program featuring an interview with David Sloan Wilson, author of a new book on evolution, *This View of Life: Completing the Darwinian Revolution*. It's about evolutionary biology, the possibility of cooperation, virtue, altruism, and our path forward as a species. One fact I wasn't aware of was that in egalitarian societies, (would that this be ours), ordinary people stop the bully (someone consumed with an inflated, dominating self, we could say.)

Then, in simple language that defied the impact it had, Wilson quoted an aboriginal mythic figure, Imu, a folkloric troublemaker, he said. Imu says: "I am greater than you, you are less than me. This is the source of all human misery." The aboriginal Imu depicts the self that needs transforming. He continues: "People are idiots, we're all sometimes a bit of an idiot from some deep place." Imu whispers: "You are special." Listen to what she means by 'special': "You are greater than other people and things. You are more important than everything and everyone. All people and things exist only to serve you." I thought, "This is why and how the self is a problem!" Wilson says that *this* needs massive checks and balances to contain the damage it can do. Today, checks and balances are eroding and bullies often rule.

This is the self that afflicts and needs transforming, not our personhood, not our sense of self, agency, empowerment, our ego capacities, our distinctive energy and voice, not how we distinctively participate in the whole. *This* – isolated, dominating, grandiosely-thinking – creates damage. Believing it stands alone, like American exceptionalism, it needs and depends on no one thing, or other, or force, greater than it. I am the captain of my ship, the master of my fate.

Now here is a view of the true self than links the individual and others in an elegant and integrative way. Psychoanalyst Christopher Bollas believes that we seek objects (people, places, things, experiences) that help us release our distinctive idiom. We learn about this *après coup*, as we live our life. We check our tracks and can see traces and impacts of what really matters to us, what infuses our activity, what we live by – based on what we hold dear.

His notion of self-experience, most of it unconscious, is intrinsically interactive with other beings. We each have our own distinctive idiom, a personal and aesthetic signature that pre-dates the environmental influences in our upbringing and needs interactive elaboration and dissemination. We seek external objects and interactions that will release this personal idiom. A simple example might be how one child is drawn early on to sounds and then to musical instruments and conducting, while another cannot get enough of throwing balls, then street games, and goes on to professional sports. Bollas describes how unconscious experience collects and comes together not only in our sleeping dreams, but also in our waking life in powerful moments of psychic intensity, powerful felt senses that are full of possible meanings. Then, by freely associating to these experienced intensities, we unpack their solidity, and a wide range of meanings and experiences emerges that seeds further moments of psychic aliveness.

Bollas provides a wonderful metaphor for thinking about the impacts we generate. He suggests we imagine watching someone moving through space in a room full of people, then imagine that we cannot see the person's body but only the effects of his actions. It is as if the person is a ghost, like in the old TV show *Topper*. The self may be insubstantial, but what impacts do we leave in our wake?

I see the personal as neither self nor no-self but rather the living creative activity of *personalization*. Unlike narcissistic self-aggrandizement, it cannot be adequately described or grasped, yet it is active, idiomatic, and without self-consciousness. I am contrasting the persona with the *person-in-action*; the latter includes reflecting, thinking, feeling, creating, imagining, intuiting – not to mention standing up, sitting down, laughing, and weeping. All of us desire to feel connected to our deepest nature, to one another, to our family, to our community, to grow beyond our small, self-preoccupied selves. We also desire to actualize our unique potentials, to represent our idiom, and contribute to the world.

In Zen as in psychotherapy practice, the aim is not to eliminate rich and distinctive character traits, but to help relieve suffering, to enhance expression of life-giving elements. I once asked a psychoanalytic colleague, after a talk she gave on the topic of transference and transcendence, whether she could imagine the absence of transference. She replied that in her experience there is always a trace of transference. Zen realization contains no transference or countertransference. In our subsequent activity, however, we let go of our experience and our attachments to it and personalize it in our everyday conduct. It is not so much that a trace of transference remains; rather, our actions are always emerging through the personal idiom. 'Dwelling nowhere,' we 'bring forth that mind,' uniquely. This 'personal' conveys the impersonal and the boundless, expressed in material and emotional particulars. Much of this process is outside our awareness, which is a blessing but can also be a curse as we will explore in the next two chapters.

This man or woman, this 'person of no-rank' comes forth afresh in each moment of life, now shopping, now making love, now brushing his teeth, now listening, now dreaming, responsively in alignment with circumstances. The person emerges from and expresses his no-self nature in the particulars of daily life. His distinctive idiom comes forward as well, unique one person from the other, but it is not on the register of affirmations of self-esteem. It reflects a sloughing off rather than a patching on or building up. It *presumes* a hardy sense of self and the capacities we have been discussing.

So let's review, from a different angle. Self is a series of shifting states, connected through the stabilizing play of illusion (illusion, *ludere*, play) of continuity, cohesiveness and coherence and cohesion. It helps us stand and learn from the discontinuities and traumas of life. A good enough, durable, resilient sense of internal coherence and cohesiveness. From this flow of shifting states, we are moment to moment constructing a more or less cohesive, coherent-enough sense of an I, a sense of personhood, continuous-enough through change and discontinuity. Via the serious play of illusion. This sponsors benevolent unfoldings: differentiation, agency, voice, capacities to bear and forebear, to suffer properly, to hold the ten thousand joys and sorrows together, to desire, to intend, to represent our idiom, our aesthetic, make use of objects with maximal aliveness, to live, and to participate vigorously.

The challenge is not to get stuck, not to identify with narrow, rigid, habitual versions of self, particular self-states, or (usually traumatic) relational configurations between them.

The person of no rank is robustly singular yet aware of her intrinsic interdependence with all beings, belonging to, and participating in, a series of widening webs. She doesn't cling to a particular version of himself, understanding that she is forming and reforming moment by moment, that she is not *a self-contained self-entity, a carve-out or a set-apart, if you will, unchanging and everlasting.* She doesn't identify with this. She's also not evacuating psychic contents, thinking that emptiness is a desirable vacuum-like state. When she does get caught up in one or another painfully looping version of self and others, the person of no-rank uses her fellows, sangha, the tradition, and her capacity to generate steady, easeful, equanimity for support, as she sees into it and lets go, returning to the immediacy at hand.

Sovereign, singular, standing on the earth on her own two feet. Differentiated, dignified, capable of bearing the pain and joy of being human, of accessing ease and rest and focus. And in her relations with the many beings, she realizes her intrinsic kinship with them, and comes home to community. Both: the interweaving of the particular being and the universal. Each point in the vast jeweled net.

UNITY, SAMENESS, DIFFERENCE AND OTHERNESS

In this section I briefly explore oneness, equality, singularity and multiplicity. The interplay of sameness and difference.

I was listening recently to a presentation on the importance of accessing a state of unity where one is not separate. I think by "separate" the presenter meant "alienated" – not belonging, apart from, isolated and disconnected from life – but I couldn't help think of difference, otherness, and how liberating it can be to recognize and come to appreciate and embrace our differences. Marion Milner, painter, psychoanalyst, and natural mystic, writes:

> Until you have, once at least, faced everything you know – the whole universe – with utter giving in, and let all that is "not you" flow over and engulf you, there can be no lasting sense of security. Only by being prepared to accept annihilation can one escape from that spiritual "abiding alone" which is in fact the truly death-like state.[6]

Surprisingly, embracing a radical otherness can free us, not from 'separateness' but from the prison of isolation and disconnection.

I thought, too, of the lifelong tasks of forging and reforging a person, a personal voice, of representing our idiom, and how critical that capacity is. This can be a fearsome task that involves mobilizing a certain aggression that spiritual practitioners tend to shy away from. We and other beings are the same and different and each presents the universal, *differently*.

I recall an early relationship. One day, in conversation, it dawned on me suddenly that my girlfriend was actually different from me. She saw things differently, she processed information differently, she expressed emotion differently. What a concept! Seeing her as different and differentiated helped me not take things quite so personally and be less self-referencing.

We're often encouraged by spiritual teachers and others to see that we're all the same, we're all one. We may be one, but we're not all the same. In the psycho-political inter-group work with warring parties by psychiatrist Vamik Volkan and others, it's clear that developing connection, empathy, a sense of unity come late in the process if at all. What's important is to listen deeply and see and appreciate (though not necessarily agree with) the ways in which our interlocutor is different from us.

After the recent death of Thich Nhat Hanh, I listened to a talk of his in which he encourages us, through our mindfulness, "to take refuge in the island of self," to come home to inner peace and rest and thereby reach the three refuges, a safe place, without the risk of being overwhelmed by waves of worry and suffering. He repeats safety many times. Returning to your heart, he says, you find benevolence, you find joy, old spiritual friends and ancestors, and other good experiences. Thay sounded lonely and appeared more grave than I remember him. Perhaps he was in some physical or emotional distress. It so happened that he had a stroke several months after this talk.

Thay was referencing the last talks of the Buddha when the Buddha was very sick. The teaching, he tells us, is *atta dipa saranam*: Atta is self; dipa is island; saranam, to come home. Come home to the island of your self. This is not the self-aggrandizing, self-absorbed, self-obsessed self, driven by anxiety and other challenging and occasionally corrosive fuels. I couldn't help but notice that his emphasis was quite in counterpoint to his early focus on interbeing.

This counterpoint exists in my Zen lineage too: In his teisho, Aitken-Roshi would talk about our being "All alone in the universe," walking "the path in royal aloneness." Hakuin Zenji wrote, "This very body is the Buddha;" in koan work, we need to present this side clearly. Simultaneously, we are "one with the universe." The cypress tree, the stones and the clouds. Dogen's words echo anew, "The mind is none other than the mountains, rivers, and great earth; the moon, the sun and the stars." In Indra's net, each jewel must shine as itself, with its own light, for the whole to be, to work harmoniously.

We must leave room for separated-ness, for uniqueness, distinctiveness, and singularity. When we say no separation, we confuse things a bit and foreclose this solitary aspect, which has its own dignity. Often, we collapse it all into 'we're all one,' into unity. When dualistic notions, of self and no self, being and not being, for example, are absent, there's a fluid interpenetration among this one here and all other beings; there's no inherent conflict between the two. This is the activity of a vigorous no-self.

Yamada Koun, who we met earlier, was a bear about cutting through delusion and realizing essential nature. But he was also a grandmother and gave us a framework for Zen practice: absorption, realization, and personalization. Each makes the others possible. What do we realize when we awaken? Many tell the story of when the Buddha was asked who he was. "I am awake," he replied. Different Buddhist schools, different stories. Awareness, non-judgmental presence, is the last word for many. This hangs together with a predilection for working with 'the mind' – referring here to how we deal with internal thoughts, feelings and bodily sensations.

I presented once with an accomplished teacher from another Buddhist lineage whom I respect very much. He is funny, open, and smart. But I realized he was focusing entirely on understanding the "mind" – a mind that was inside the head or the brain. I didn't hear the birds, feel the wind, see the clouds and mountains. "What is revealed when the mind is liberated from its fetters?" I asked. "Awareness," he responded. Zen cooking is different. Old ancestor Yamada made it clear: "Zen is just sitting down, just standing up, just laughing, just weeping." Next time we taught, we were less polite and more inclined to face and play with our differences. The stew we cooked up was more flavorful.

Once I was sitting in silence with dear friends, a silence that was their mode of worship. After about 45 minutes, there was a rumbling that shook the building. Then it ebbed, and after fifteen seconds or so it ended. There was sharing during and after the silence, but no one mentioned the quake. I said, "I couldn't help but notice the great mother shudder." People spoke but nary a mention of the tremors. Was the rumbling a distraction to the silent, 'inner' reflection? Their clear awareness'? Were people oblivious? Ignoring it? I was thrilled during those fifteen seconds: The Dharma talk for the day!

Someone asked great master Yunmen, "What is my I?" Yunmen responded, "Strolling in the mountains, enjoying the rivers." Don't take this as 'outer!' When self-preoccupation falls away, we come upon a fathomless silence, roughly equivalent to the Awareness mentioned earlier. Nothing to say and nothing left unsaid. Discursive mind is light years gone.

In Zen, there's another step. How do you present essential nature in particulars? "Take a step from the top of a hundred-foot pole." Don't get stuck in empty oneness. Persevere and, unpredictably, our grip on dualistic formulations – self-other, enlightened-deluded, self-no-self, inner-outer, 'mind' and Awareness – gives way. What do we discover?

"Arp, arp, arp!" This bag of skin may define my human contours but it no longer confines. Is this enlightened? Deluded? Even equating it with *suchness* is miles off. Yet, a person of no-rank is activated.

A revered Buddhist teacher said that when we are truly silent, there is a hard-to-hear sound. He suggested this might be "The sound of one hand," a reference to a Zen koan. In Haleakala crater on Maui the silence is awesome, but "The sound of one hand" is not something located beneath the threshold of ordinary human hearing.

> In speech you hear its silence.
> The great way has opened and there are no obstacles.

Yongjia Xuanjue does not simply mean that an awakened person speaks in a measured, peaceful manner. When the way opens wide, what becomes apparent? The 'other' is no other than myself. Except that there is nothing to be called self or other; it is not on that register. Immeasurable and ungraspable, it is presented in vivid particulars. How is it personalized? Who stands up, sits down? Who laughs and weeps?

In "Tea at the Palaz of Hoon," Wallace Stevens coveys the flavor of Zen awakening:

> I was the world
> in which I walked
> and what I saw
> Or heard or felt came not
> but from myself
> And there I found myself more truly and
> more strange.[7]

A person of no rank, our true nature, is a jewel of no-price. It can't be bought or sold, it's not on the register of commerce or conceptual formulations. Shining distinctively and intimate with all beings, we call it the Jeweled Net of Indra. The person of no-rank lives in poverty and participates in the riches. How? The great layman P'ang said,

> In every place, there's no hindrance...
> [My] supernatural powers and marvelous activity –
> Drawing water and carrying firewood.

In personalizing Zen realization, this shore, Samsara, and the other shore, Nirvana, fall away. A person of no-rank awakens. The sense of self remains our psychological lattice work, our ego capacities are intact; they serve and don't intrude. We live Buddha's dream, first hand. Self-interest is not eradicated. Rather,

> Each bird, bud, midge, mole, atom, crystal, (is) of total importance in itself. As in the notes of a great symphony, nothing (is) large or small, nothing of more or less importance to the whole...[8]

Human beings included. Emptiness as vacancy cannot capture this. No concept, no blueprint can. 'Potential space,' coined by a psychoanalyst, gives us a sense. 'Limitless belonging,' coined by a Benedictine monk, is also evocative. Self-interest and collective benefit here do not oppose each other. What benefits me most deeply brings benefit to others. When the other blossoms, I am enriched.

Language matters. Being 'separate' is not our fundamental delusion. Differentiation is a necessity. What plagues us is pervasive isolation and disconnection. Often originating in trauma, they come with a helping of repudiation – turning away from anguish that is difficult to face. Separateness is vital; you individuate as a unique person with a distinctive voice and a sense of agency: an agent of compassion. The goddess Indra needs each point in her fabled Jeweled Net, each being, to realize not only its inherent unity with all beings, but to shine unselfconsciously with its own distinctiveness. To vigorously bring forth her true no self nature for the benefit of all.

We can call this symbiosis 'no-mind.' Some equate the mind with everything going on in their full-to-bursting head, everything they're dancing too fast to engineer better. Wipe the dust off the old *Diamond Sutra*: "Dwelling 'nowhere' bring forth that mind." Dwelling in a frustrating work meeting with an annoying coworker or a community riven by hatred, bring forth the mind where you and all beings *interare*.

Certainly, there are dangers in using the term 'true self.' Nowadays it can mean almost anything. It can refer to my alter ego, a way of being I protect and never allow to show, or wanting to do work that's fascinated me, say being a designer. Does true equate with good? What about when someone equates true self with wanting to rule the world, or at least the equities market? Or with wiping out an entire people. True can mean being vulnerable; we can wish for conditions that permit something new, something authentic. True self is a slippery and saturated term. Yet, in today's world, rarity makes the heart grow fonder: *True* is so compelling that I devote significant space to its permutations, connections, and liberation.

What about good and evil? Is a true person of no rank value-free? What about the ethics of your no-mind awakened mind? Taking each element by itself is futile: How can we wall off *Dhyana, Prajna* and *Sila* (meditation, insight, and awakened activity) from one another? Abandon the search for the silver bullet blueprint, the all-encompassing algorithm. Anything you and I craft is subject to changing conditions on the ground. Remember, it takes a full real human being to personalize Buddha's dream and bring it to life. And there's the rub. And the open gate.

In the next chapter, I examine archetypes of Buddhist practice and introduce a modern one drawn from 'America's favorite pastime,' baseball. I also describe what gets lost in translation between our insights and our daily life activity of embodying them.

2

BUDDHA'S DREAM

How does a "fully functioning human" being live? (Winnicott). How does a person exemplify the "Great Functioning?" (Yun-men). In *Mahayana* Buddhism (great vehicle), the archetype is the *bodhisattva*, in *Theravada* Buddhism (school of the elders), the *arhant*. Mahayanists used to refer to Theravadins as the *Hinayana* (lesser vehicle) school. "Lesser" because they focused on their own liberation. "Greater" because it's a big tent, a big project, working toward the liberation of all beings. What hubris! As we know, all vehicles shall be towed. I wonder if *mensch* would be a possibility. In this book, I propose a "true *person* of no rank," an agent of compassion.

Ideals cut in different ways. They can inspire, and they can tyrannize. They are dreams that animate practice, working behind the scenes as internalized guides to live by. No matter how useful, however, it is important to stay open to learning from experience and revising them when useful.

In baseball, the ideal is a five-tool player. He can hit for average, hit for power, field, throw and run. The greatest of these rare players in the years I was growing up was Willie Mays. (Yankee fans of my era will claim it was Mickey Mantle, but they're mistaken.) A five-tool player is accomplished, superbly well-rounded and integrated. Always learning and refining. And the really great ones have a sixth tool: They make others better. The pillars of the Buddhist dream are *Dhyana* (*samadhi* or focused meditation), *Prajna*, (direct, unmediated insight), and *Sila* (precepts). Ideally, these work in concert; each supporting the others, they interpenetrate. When they are in harmony, wisdom and compassion arise. Playfully we could call a Buddhist practitioner where these five elements work in concert and who exhibits durable traits of wisdom and compassion, a Buddhist five-tool player. The Bodhisattva is an awakened being, is awaken-ing, and awakens others. Baseball's five-tool player, we might say, is well-integrated, integrate-ing, and helps others become better integrated, well-rounded, and aligned.

I find it useful to think of Sila not only as precepts but also as awakened action, action that redounds to the benefit of the many. But what's become clear is that strong steady dhyana and scintillating prajna do not necessarily lead to awakened action – to the contrary. Dhyana, prajna and sila don't reliably generate wisdom and compassion. Something can get lost in translation. The alchemy that generates wisdom and compassion (as traits, not simply states), working seamlessly in concert, doesn't materialize.

In the early days of the Maui Zendo, after *sesshin*, we would pile into the Zendo van and drive to Baldwin Beach to swim, hang out, and eat junk food. Aitken Roshi would usually come along. Once, after a swim, I asked him, "Why is it that some residents who experience *kensho* (enlightenment) often continue to treat others in the same thought-less ways they did before their experience?" He replied, "They must not be really doing zazen." Even as a green student, I felt that his response raised questions. Was it simply a matter of practicing more diligently? Our senior Japanese teacher, Yamada Koun Roshi, taught that Zen was "the perfection of character," but it didn't seem to be. The *transfer of training*, a term I heard in an education class at college, did not seem to be reliable. There wasn't an automatic alignment of dhyana, prajna, and sila. Although compassion did rise in the hearts of many who had *kensho*, this didn't seem to translate into mutually beneficial conduct or observable character change. Yamada Roshi's schema for the Zen train-ing – absorption (*samadhi*), realization (*kensho* or enlightenment), and personalization (embodying the experience of awakening in the particu-lars of one's life while letting go of all traces of attachment) – seemed to be impediments as we made it our own and lived it.

Yamada Roshi was once asked how a respected leader in the Rinzai sect could have committed suicide; he replied that the master must have not been fully enlightened. I don't agree. The difficulty is not solely in the practitioner: the way the path is conceived can stand examination. At the end of his life, concerned about growing international conflict, longing for world peace, and aware of discord in his community re-garding his eventual succession, Yamada Roshi made what I find to be a remarkable turnaround and integration. Given his own dramatic and profound enlightenment experience, he had always emphatically taught the importance of developing and refining the "enlightened eye," insight into our empty essential nature (Prajna). Compassion and awakened activity, "the perfection of character," would ensue naturally. But, in his later years he saw that this was not necessarily so and wrote that, just as important – perhaps even more important than enlightenment and its refinement – was the cultivation of spiritual qualities like kindness, compassion, mutual respect, and understanding.

Early on Aitken Roshi privileged dhyana, Yamada Roshi, prajna. This natural alignment among the three pillars would work, but only if the student's zazen was stronger or the Zen master's insight was deeper. However, I've seen many students and teachers with strong zazen and others with deep insight who conduct themselves in ways that generate distress, hurt, and even harm for others, and for themselves. Further, strong zazen can exist in isolation like, say, a pair of big forearms on an otherwise thin body. Deep insight can be present without particularly solid zazen or without embodied alignment with precepts. And someone can diligently study hundreds of Buddhist precepts without a glimmer of insight into our true nature. And even if all three are active, the alchemy to wisdom and compassion can go in and out of alignment.

The disconnects among dhyana, prajna, and sila are not uncommon. Realizing their symbiosis in ourselves, and especially in our relational lives, is quite challenging. As news of the ethical misconduct and boundary violations on the part of Zen and other spiritual teachers spread, it was painful yet instructive for me to learn about teachers respected for their insight, practice, and virtue, some of them my friends, acting in ways detrimental and harmful to their students.

In the Buddhist dream, wisdom and compassion are the natural fruit, the ripening of dhyana, prajna and sila. The Bodhisattva of compassion, Kwan-Yin, at deep rest, hears the sounds of suffering and responds. Does this happen automatically? Is there a trickle-down effect? Koan study in the Diamond Sangha or other koan traditions may or may not assist us in embodying our insight that all beings are, by nature, awakened.

Beginning in the 1970s, a number of Buddhist practitioners, some but not all of us therapists, began to notice that even the most 'enlightened' teachers were leaving harm in their wake: ethical transgressions and abuse of sex, money and power. It began to appear that something was being 'lost in translation,' that is, in the embodiment of their realization. Many of us had mistakenly believed that one or more enlightenment experiences, with the direct insight and compassion that accompanied them, would assure, in a variant of the trickle-down effect, the embodiment of that realization, lasting the rest of one's life, in all places, situations, and times.

The title of Jack Kornfield's 2001 book, *After the Ecstasy the Laundry*, humorously captures something of this apparent paradox. Many however, took the title to mean that after you faced and 'cleaned up' your 'dirty' laundry, referring (sadly) to unaddressed emotional issues, for example, that you would lead an unfettered life, free of suffering. More than a few students still believe this. But personal, familial, and planetary suffering persist; "they rise endlessly," as we recite in our vows.

Ram Dass said that it took his entire adult life, including a stroke, to become like the person his legions of followers thought him to be when he returned, shining and beaming, from India. That's certainly been the experience of many Zen practitioners and teachers; integrating whatever insight or realization may have been gleaned into our day-to-day lives is a lifetime affair. This speaks to bread and butter emotional work; personal, relational and trauma work. Perhaps the brighter the light, the wider the shadow. Can we be blinded by the light?

Many (perhaps most) Western Buddhist teachers have by now been in some form of psychological work. Sanghas and residential centers began weaving in group support work years ago. I have come to see that zazen, realization (direct insight or kensho), and precepts slip in and out of alignment quite often, especially when one of these three dimensions is overemphasized. This can leave unexamined pockets of afflictive experience that cause suffering and harm. However, this has not, with a few exceptions, been reflected in the contemporary narratives, the organizing stories of the Zen practitioner and the Zen teacher and their 'continuing education' in the Way. I'm aiming for a more inclusive, integrative and experience-near narrative with ideals and archetypes that align.

What are the hidden factors that throw a wrench in Buddha's dream? I think of the Broadway musical, *A Funny Thing Happened on the Way to the Forum*. What happens? What doesn't happen? Why? Something remains unactualized; let's call it wise and compassionate action. There are potholes, pitfalls, stumbling blocks, hindrances, fetters. Many are hidden, some hidden in plain sight. Ethical transgressions are harmful in themselves, but my point is that they are also symptoms of more generalized lacunae in our practice and in the narrative of the Buddhist dream.

We often don't know the impacts of our actions –
our conduct, speech, and thought.

We tend to assume they will be benevolent because we're practicing regularly, continuing to refine our insight and internalizing and living our vows. It doesn't occur to us that some effects we're engendering may be quite different from what we intended. The blind spot, regarding say the abuse scandals, is not just that some teachers are malignant narcissists, sociopaths, predators, addicts, or all of the above. Raising our collective emotional IQ about psychopathology helps. But it's a subset of a higher-level problem. We don't understand unconscious emotional communication and unconscious motivation. The latter can highjack the activity of purifying our intention, something we'll explore in more detail in the next chapter.

When Zen came west, the most fruitful encounters were with feminism, racism, ecology, social and political action, and western psychology. But the 'funny thing that happens on the ways to the forum' (to liberation) is that liberation occurs on two tracks. Spiritual experience and growth on the one hand and emotional experience and growth on the other inter-are. Both paths, Zen and psychotherapy, involve the activities of letting go and coming forth, although the two disciplines have tended traditionally to privilege one aspect more than the other. For purposes of comparison, the two approaches may be thought of as containing different 'proportions' of each activity. The image of a double helix captures something of their dynamic relationship. Each strand is discrete, yet each intersects the other and, in so doing, changes the other and is itself changed. Working in concert, the whole evolves in the direction of deeper aliveness, truth, integrated self-knowledge, and compassion for others.

Now, western Buddhists have explored and continue to explore emotions, emotional intelligence, emotional regulation, relationships, and so on. They know about transference, countertransference, projection, group process, and are discovering character disorders, malignant narcissism and sociopathy among them, and addictions. But there's something missing, something crucial that's escaping our purview.

I once excitedly told an old dharma friend a prospective title for my first book, *The Bliss Body and the Unconscious*. A long-time former therapist and experienced Buddhist teacher, her spontaneous yet uncharacteristically deadpan response spoke volumes, "I like the Bliss Body part." For dharma practitioners, unconscious usually connotes being unaware, even clueless, except perhaps when it refers to an athlete: He was 'in the zone,' just 'unconscious.' We put a premium on conscious practice. We do not understand or make room for this wild card, the unconscious. We study koans and stories about 'not knowing,' but we don't appreciate just how much is being communicated beneath our conscious awareness.

Remember the Dalai Lama's response to a question: "When I'm uncertain or distressed, I look inside and check my motivation. Motivation is key. If I am motivated by afflictive emotions, I work on myself. If I am motivated by wholesome emotions, if that is clear after careful examination, I don't care what anybody thinks [about me]."

Working on himself involves some kind of conscious introspection. But we don't see that *if conscious introspection alone sufficed to transform the factors that engender suffering, then we would have long ago achieved individual as well as collective peace, freedom, and justice (*the collective manifestations of dhyana, prajna and sila*).

If we want to know someone we should probably ask their partner, or their dog or cat. Partners and pets often pick up on what's really happening, what the person is really conveying, and can see factors we (and s/he) can't. Buddhists have read about emotional intelligence, but we know next to nothing about *unconscious emotional intelligence*, specifically, for our purposes, unconscious emotional communication in the relational field. I may say I'm happy as a clam, but to my co-workers, it's hidden in plain sight that I'm miserable and beginning to make them miserable. But I remain clueless. Osel Tenzin 'knew' he had so transcended his conditioning and his biology that his impacts could only be benevolent. But his sexual activity made scores of people ill, and some died. This is an extreme example, yes, but it's illustrative.

Yasutani Roshi, my great grandfather in the Dharma, was asked what our fundamental delusion was. He responded, "That you are there and I am here." In Zen (and other traditions of) awakening, this gulf dissolves: We are one *and* unique, no opposition at all. Dualities such as subject and object, inner and outer are simply absent. Then in our daily lives, we participate in a range of relationships with others (not Others), where there is another being, different from us, sometimes right in our face. How do we respond? How does Bodhisattva Avalokitesvara with her many hands and eyes respond? Bernie Glassman Roshi used an interesting schema: First, 'don't know;' second, bear witness; and third, act with spontaneous compassion. Aitken Roshi in *The Mind of Clover*, says that clover has no choice but to respond benevolently, giving its life as nutrition to the earth. But human beings have a choice. And, something can get mired or foreclosed. Spontaneity is valued in Zen, but it needs to be the informed kind.

IDEALS

Our ideals can trip us up. I used to believe the conventional wisdom that bodhisattvas forswore their own complete enlightenment until all beings were free; now I see it is mistaken. Someone who sees deeply, in this very moment, that his own happiness develops in concert with the happiness and liberation of others – and whose actions arise from the ground of this realization – such a person is an awakening being, a bodhisattva. As the other blossoms, I blossom and find joy. As I deepen, the other benefits.

In Zen, we vow to "save all beings." This doesn't imply converting. From the beginning, "All beings by nature are Buddha." The Dalai Lama told a group of Western Buddhist teachers, "When you speak about helping, it sounds a bit like a one-way street, you helping others. In Tibetan, the word 'compassion' has no direction, it is omnidirectional." The point he was making was that compassion includes myself, the agent of compassion, a point in the multicentered Net of Indra.

A friend inquired if Gandhi's aim in settling in the village and serving the villagers as best he could was purely humanitarian. Gandhi replied, "I am here to serve no one else but myself, to find my own self-realization through the service of these village folk." An Aboriginal elder told some visitors, "If you have come to liberate me, turn around and go home. But if you see that your liberation and mine are bound up together, let's see what we can do."

This true no self, a person of no rank,
is no shrinking violet or self-sacrificing martyr.

IN AND OUT OF ALIGNMENT

Returning to the interplay of conscious and unconscious, there have been many spiritually informed systems and practices for navigating the challenges of embodiment: active listening, nonviolent communication, and counsel being just a few. But there are forces at play we are unaware of. Knowing about trauma and dissociation and helping others heal doesn't exempt us from experiencing them, periodically, activated in real life relational situations. Why? Because it's unconscious.

Here are a few examples. A seasoned Buddhist teacher with deep insight into essential nature makes the point at a seminar that there is fundamentally "nothing to know." As he says this, however, he conveys precisely the opposite: that he *does* know and the others do not. He is not aware that this is happening, but others are. A group of seasoned teachers meet for a week around the question of succession. Interpersonal tensions emerge, and there is expert facilitation. The meeting ends with unanimous agreement regarding its efficacy. Within days, things explode, and schisms are rampant.

Teachers we know and trust and love shock us with actions we never would have thought possible. I brought reports of sexual boundary violations that I'd heard about to a trusted friend of the teacher in question, a friend who was skilled, trusted, a teacher himself, and psychologically astute. He brushed off the reports. Several years later a woman came forth with new complaints and a committee was formed of the teacher's best Dharma friends, all widely known, respected and psychologically minded, to hear the reports first-hand and hear too from the teacher. They were shocked.

Why should they be shocked? One reason often not considered is that they weren't open to the power of unconscious emotional forces. Denial was strong, of course, but more, the teachers on the committee had disavowed what they were seeing. They had unconsciously deceived themselves. It was quite the object lesson. One of them, in fact the person who initially brushed it off, now frequently tells the story about how, despite having a powerful enlightenment experience, teachers can act ignorantly and harmfully and deceitfully.

Here's an example around power where this explosive quality also manifested. A beloved, wise teacher known for reconciliation suddenly turned the tables on a large group of her students and engineered a power grab, shocking those who had been responsible for spreading her teaching and for her renown.

An older and much beloved teacher who emphasized clear awareness of moment-to-moment experience began to have second thoughts about having given transmission to some students. Finally, he took back the authorizations, scolding the teachers and prompting shock for many at how he seemed to have changed so.

These aspects of our character aren't manifest, sometimes for decades. Until they are. The key point I want to convey is that even those who are psychologically minded, well-versed in emotional and relational life (and even aware of unconscious experience) are subject to them. Why? Because they're unconscious! We do well to learn about and ally ourselves with the unconscious; it can assist us to accomplish the Buddhist project of purifying (refining) our intention and liberating all beings. Unacknowledged, it wreaks havoc and undermines our practice.

If the double helix is a metaphor for how intertwined and mutually influencing spiritual and emotion experience are, the image may also serve to describe the relationship between conscious meditation practices and unconscious experience: a dynamic relationship where each strand is discrete, yet each intersects the other and, in so doing, changes the other and is itself changed. Working in concert, the whole evolves in the direction of deeper aliveness, truth, integrated self-knowledge, and compassion for others.

We need to learn to cast a ray of darkness into the matter, beginning with accepting that we really do not know and that something is bound to get lost or twisted in our most human daily lives. More on addressing this through tracking the traces of the impacts of our actions in the next chapter.

BLOWS

Freud thinks that we have been dealt "severe blows to human self-love" by three revolutions in human thought. First, Copernicus discovered that the earth is not the center of the universe, and neither is man. Then, Darwin showed that humans are subject to the same laws as microorganisms, so we are not so special after all. Finally, Freud's (1915) elaboration of the unconscious added insult to injury by demonstrating that we are not in control of even our own self-experience. "The ego," he writes, "is not master in its own house." And what about the Buddha? He invites us to discover that our house is not what we thought, that what and whom we take as real may be a case of mistaken identity. We may be more vast and more interconnected than we ever imagined – and less substantial.

Many Buddhists cringe when they hear about the unconscious. Recall my Dharma friend's response to the title idea, *The Bliss Body and the Unconscious*, "I like the bliss body part." It made me laugh, and when she asked why I was laughing, her question reinforced why I was writing the book. Perhaps, it confirmed Freud's "not master in our own house" hypothesis. Another Buddhist teacher friend, a fellow basketball fan, finds it easy to speak about Michael Jordan or other superstars being "unconscious" or "in the zone" during a game, but he also refers to moments of being unreflective as being "unconscious." On the other hand, psychoanalysts speak of "getting unconscious together" when describing a workgroup in which the shared reverie of group members is mined. It was the psychoanalyst James Grotstein who suggested that we "cast a ray of darkness" into perplexing experience because attempts to consciously understand sometimes yield only predictable formulations of limited value.

I have come to believe that Buddhist meditators tend to overprivilege conscious introspection, and for that matter consciousness. They think the unconscious is still just the *Id*, the repository of forbidden sexual and aggressive wishes that reduces humans to a bundle of blind impulses. It gets under their skin. I think most don't appreciate just how far the unconscious has come. As Buddhists we are aware of emotional intelligence but far less of *unconscious* emotional intelligence.

UNCONSCIOUS EXPERIENCE

In his early work, Freud thought that we each have in our brain a "transmitter" and a "receiver." He believed that humans communicated *emotionally* without conscious mediation. But he never pursued this idea. So we still think of the Freudian unconscious as a repository of repressed wishes, primarily sexual and aggressive; the proverbial 'teeming cauldron.' Two people who have built on and expanded Freud's original idea are psychoanalyst Christopher Bollas and neuropsychologist Allan Schore.

You'll recall that Bollas describes an unconscious not characterized by repression of forbidden desires. He calls the unconscious the "unthought known," an emotional field so radically interconnected that it is the analyst who often receives the patient's thoughts, feeling, sensations, and images before the patient herself thinks about or even becomes aware of them. Bollas' notion of "self-experience," most of it unconscious, is intrinsically interactive with objects in the outside world. We each, he writes, have our own distinctive *idiom*, a personal and aesthetic signature that predates the environmental influences in our upbringing. A version of the true self. We seek, again unconsciously, external objects and experiences that will help us express this personal idiom.

Bollas further describes how unconscious experience coalesces, not only in our sleeping dreams, but also in our waking life, in especially compelling moments of psychic intensity – like a powerful felt sense. By freely associating in these intense moments, we can unpack their hidden dimensions, and an array of meanings can emerge. These are expressed in interpersonal and collective situations and provide the "raw material" for new moments of psychic intensity.

Another kind of unconscious experience is animated by the impacts of developmental and adult-onset trauma, individual and collective, that cannot be processed and don't find their way into our usual ('declarative' or 'explicit') memory. They're not encoded symbolically and can't be worked over using language. They remain deeply buried and may be reactivated somatically. Dissociated traumatic residues, though unconscious to the person, *are* conveyed to others through emotional communication. The results may be confusing, painful, or shocking. We may think we're fine, benevolent even, when what we are actually conveying is of a quite different character. It takes an 'other' to help us learn from this experience.

This unconscious has been a major focus of Allan Schore's life work. "The construct of the unconscious," Schore writes, "is now being used to describe essential implicit, spontaneous, rapid, and involuntary processes that act beneath levels of conscious awareness." The earliest relationship with another human is "mediated by unconscious right brain-to-right brain attachment communications between the mother (or other primary caregiver) and infant." This bond is characterized by rapid emotional communications between the mother's right brain unconscious and the infant's emerging right brain unconscious. These early affective experiences during critical periods of development profoundly influence the development of the right brain and psychic structures that process unconscious information. They are "proto-conversations between two brains." Schore provides data that he says demonstrate that the right brain is the psychobiological substrate of Freud's preverbal communicative unconscious.

He cites researchers who demonstrate that the implicit, nonconscious process of non-verbal affective cues in infancy "is repetitive, automatic, provides quick categorization and decision-making, and operates outside the realm of focal attention and verbalized experience." In all interactions (face-to-face as well as body-to-body), "the mother is implicitly shaping her infant's unconscious mind, which develops before the conscious mind." When these mutually synchronized social interactions go awry, when the interactive regulation provided by the caregiver is not functioning well enough, the infant can become overwhelmed by unmanageable states. These are then often dissociated in the interest of psychic survival.

This "still-face" experiment conducted by infant researcher Edward Tronick involves a baby and parent (in this case the mother) sitting facing each other. The mother begins by playing with her baby, smiling and talking. Then she then turns away. The mother shows a still face, not responding to her baby for two minutes. At first the infant looks confused. He does everything he can to elicit a response, pointing and smiling and looking around the room. As his efforts to connect are ignored, he becomes distressed and frustrated. He begins crying and then screeching. He even bites his own hand. Some babies physically collapse. It's difficult watch the baby dissolve emotionally. As the experiment draws to a close, the baby becomes withdrawn and hopeless, and no longer tries to get his mother's attention.

After the still-face part of the experiment, the mother becomes expressive and responsive again, playing and talking with her baby. Their reunion is joyful and a relief to the baby, who becomes able once again to regulate his emotions and play again. But imagine these episodes, without the joyful reunion, being frequently part of an infant's ongoing experience (and more, if they are unpredictable). Such a baby will not easily recoup her capacity to self-regulate and to play and connect. Withdrawal, numbing, or other dysregulated states may result. Dissociation is one possible way such children stay alive, at a great price.

Here's another example, this one from the consulting room. A patient was speaking about her traumatic experience of abuse. As she shared more details, her voice became increasingly distant, as if she were reporting a faraway scene. At the very same time, I began to feel a deep sadness and my eyes began to well up with tears. The patient had become quite used to emptying herself of unbearable emotions. In this case I was the one who got to experience her dissociated feelings. I happened to be a more receptive container than her parents. Our drive to heal is strong, so this dissociation wasn't solely avoidant; it was a communication without words.

This dynamically interconnected and communicative relational/emotional unconscious puts living flesh on Indra's Jeweled Net.

I've come to see that unconscious experience may also function in Zen practice in a liberating way. Let's take, "What is Buddha," a common theme in koan study. As Zen students, we often begin by trying to figure the koan out with logical reasoning. Once that abates, the inquiry drops to another level. We're not thinking of the answer. The question, word, or phrase, held patiently like a confusing set of emotional or bodily experiences, asks itself, works on itself, unconsciously. The mechanism is comparable to when we have a difficult decision to make. We go back and forth with mental ping pong, make lists of the pros and cons, and finally we hit an impasse. We give up. But we remain profoundly curious, and the question continues operating beneath the level of consciousness. And then, one day, out of the blue, it's as clear as day, as if we always knew it, as if it had always been so. In a moment that takes no time at all, we break free and know things without intermediary. The realm of play opens. Koan work involves an unconscious, inquiring creativity.

The foundational Zen story tells how the Buddha, after weeks of sitting under the Bodhi tree inquiring into the roots of human suffering, opened his eyes one dawn to see the morning star. Legend has it that he exclaimed, "Now I see that all beings by nature are enlightened from the beginning. It is only because of their ignorance and attachments that they cannot bear witness to this." What did the Buddha realize when he saw the morning star? I don't discount sudden, unmediated, penetrating insight; to the contrary. I have no argument with enlightenment; only with our thinking it's like Mr. Clean – good for counters, dishes, floors and clothes. I want to suggest an alternative narrative to awakening through dialogue with a teacher.

The Zen master does not 'enlighten' the student, as many Zen stories seem to imply. Zen dialogue may be similar to how new experience is intersubjectively (jointly, mutually, in concert) generated in psychotherapy. What if, rather than enlightening the student, it worked something like this: The Zen teacher "holds in trusteeship" (Grotstein) the transformative insight into the identity of *samsara* and *nirvana* – form and emptiness – a realization the student cannot yet "dream" or realize for him or herself. In time, as the student's practice deepens, the student conveys, via unconscious communication, a growing "readiness," a ripening. Then, at an opportune moment, the teacher, moved nonconsciously, intuitively in sync with the student, says a word or makes an action that helps reveal to the student what has been all the while apparent but unavailable.

Avalokitesvara sees the sounds of suffering and is moved to bear witness; she responds in alignment with the painful circumstances. A premium is placed on spontaneity, but who's to say my response with the traumatized patient was not some blind impulsive action whose effects may be deleterious? I like to call the experienced student or teacher's responsive action a 'tutored' spontaneity. Some responsive action needs to be thoughtfully considered, but in the Zen narrative, awakened action, precepts-in-action if you will, emerges, like sudden prajna, with immediacy. There are elements that train this kind of response in alignment but finally, the response is nonconscious, not deliberated upon in mental ping-pong. And, there evolves a certain trust in this nonconscious response. But beware, complacency and even hubris (it too, unconscious) can lead to potholes more than a few have fallen into. We'll get into this, and explore ways to prevent and get out of such potholes, in the next chapter, Motive Force.

> *A true person of no rank, infused with Avalokitesvara's boundless compassion, lives in and with and makes good use of unconscious processes (in a binocular manner). They are partners in liberation.*

STANDING, UNDERSTANDING AND TURNING TOWARD TRUTH

How important is the ability to endure and learn from afflictive and confusing mental, emotional and bodily experiences? Sylvia Boorstein, a senior Buddhist teacher who used to practice psychotherapy, was talking with her husband, Seymour, a psychoanalyst. He had just returned from the office and was telling her how much he enjoyed working and understanding things. She replied, "Me, too, but sometimes I like it when I can just *stand* things." Standing and understanding – each is part and parcel of psychoanalysis and Buddhist practice. Standing is an element of *dhyana*, understanding of *prajna*. The capacity to hold and be with our immediate experience develops during – and is paradoxically necessary for – both practices. Containment and insight develop in concert and build on one another. We begin where we are and develop the tools to do the work and play as we go. There is a lively interplay between standing and understanding. Can we bear what psychoanalysts Meltzer and Harris call the "full thought" or what Kazantzakis, in *Zorba the Greek,* calls "the full catastrophe"? Can we live our immediate experience fully and come through alive, even enlivened?

One meaning for *dukkha*, suffering, is difficulty. It is difficult to face suffering, within and without. Developing the capacity to bear, endure, and (with)stand generates a certain meditative or emotional muscle, a hardiness, openness, integrative potential, and what Keats called "negative capacity." Joko Beck described the ABC's of Zen as A Bigger Container. But it is possible to let go of troublesome experience, leapfrog into a state of samadhi, and then break through into awakening, a vast, infinite container, without well-developed capacities mentioned above. Engaging and not turning away from discomfort, emotional or relational pain builds capacities: a sense of self, ego functions, humility, a sense of agency and personhood. These then become the invisibly functioning framework, the backcloth, that permits us to *truly* let go, to unhitch attentionally from afflictive patterning and actualize peace and liberation. We can learn to practice with pain; to tolerate not knowing, to stand in the spaces, to bear the "beams of love," (Blake). But here's the tricky part; this is not just an act of will or a conscious training; it implies an inner turning toward what may or may not be present.

British psychoanalyst Neville Symington, traces this "turning" back to early life. He proposes that, in response to trauma, the infant either chooses or repudiates an internal object (internalized other) that he names "the lifegiver." In choosing the lifegiver, the infant creates it, and with it a source of creative emotional life. In repudiating it, the infant unconsciously identifies with fragmented aspects of traumatizing situations and people and encloses him or herself in a narcissistic envelope. Symington calls the repudiation the narcissistic option and sees it as the crux of much psychological disturbance. He sets it in contradistinction to the creative, life-giving, truth-affirming internal choice.

Repudiating the lifegiver, Symington writes, is rooted in anxiety about the devastating potential of psychic pain. In describing this process, he is placing value on the capacity to tolerate frustration, to 'not know.' Attributing intentionality even to the infant, (and how much more so adults), he emphasizes the unconscious dimension of this choice and speaks of evading or turning away from. When we decide to turn away from pain, we may turn away from life as well. While this can be reactive and survival-driven, the protective structures we develop take on a life of their own. But they can also become quite obstructive, even malevolent, forces to be reckoned with.

The Hebrew word *teshuvah* means "repentance" but more fundamentally refers to a turning toward truth. The act of taking refuge, in

Buddhism, may likewise be translated as "I turn toward" or "I find my home in." As parents, we use this instinctive capacity to tune in to our infant and distinguish the quality and meaning of his cry, which informs our response.

To recap, capacities to feel and manage feeling, among others, are gained through mutual synchronized proto-conversations with a responsive, containing caregiver. These are informed by and in turn grow the sense of self, personhood, agency, of empowerment, which spawn a distinctive voice, a signature or idiom. Without them, we're like Zen zombies. They only obtrude when they're impoverished or threatened. Otherwise, they leave us alone, and work, invisibly. Then they are no self, no person, no agent, just the harmonious working of the psyche-soma, the fully functioning human being whose life is the Great Functioning: just standing up, just sitting down, just laughing, just weeping. Forgetting the self in the act of uniting with and responding to the activity at hand.

Cultivating these mutually enhancing elements helps facilitate actualization, to restore what's been lost in translation. In the next chapter, "Motive Force," we'll see how it also contributes to purifying our motivation, cultivating our intention, our *bodhicitta*, the aspiration for enlightenment for ourselves and for all beings – the Buddhist project.

3

MOTIVE FORCE

In this chapter, we'll investigate what 'gets lost in translation' – what can scuttle the Buddhist dream, contribute to a misalignment among dhyana, prajna, and sila, and lead to a misfiring in the alchemy that brings about the stable traits of wisdom and compassion. We explore how Zen practice is the refinement of the person (perfection of character, purification) and how liberation and its embodiment are informed by a relational ethic. We unpack intention, look afresh at the law of cause and effect, and introduce the original idea of psychic fuels, motivational energies that animate our moment-to-moment conduct and interactions, often without our being aware of them. We describe the value of a subtle integrative awareness of the moment-to-moment influence of these psychic fuels. The free expression of a person of no-rank, our true no-self, does not exist in a vacuum, free of values: as we transform anguish, we develop a tutored spontaneity and cultivate a more nuanced awareness of the impacts of our conduct. This brings our practice, understanding, and actions into alignment, restoring the intrinsic intersectionality of the Buddhist dream. We depend on our awareness, trust our insight and practice, and we also turn to numerous others to help us in our ongoing awakening.

> For all the harmful karma, ever created by me since of old
> On account of my beginningless greed, hatred, and ignorance,
> Born of my conduct, speech, and thought
> I now atone openly and fully.[9]

When I throw a stone into a lake, ripples radiate out omnidirectionally. As a child, I would follow them until they blended back in and the water's surface became smooth again. As an adult, I see that these ripples have a life of their own, a long life, and we often don't know and can't predict what that stone and those ripples will leave in their wake.

On November 19, 2005 I spoke at San Quentin Prison at a Save the Peacemaker rally, urging then-Governor Arnold Schwarzenegger to grant clemency to Stanley 'Tookie' Williams, the founder of a deadly gang, who publicly and repeatedly renounced violence and urged others to do so. Tookie would speak from his own experience about the reality of gang and prison life, countering its deadly glamorization. He dedicated his last twelve years to promoting *Ahimsa*, non-harming, the heart of Buddhism. I said,

> We do no harm, in word, thought, and deed, when we understand in our marrow that the other is none other than myself, that each and every being, by nature is awakened and sacred. This seeing is the activity of wisdom and leads to compassionate action.
>
> Ahimsa, wisdom, and compassion are not theological concepts, but ways to live in the world that bring peace, well-being and joy. It's up to each of us to bring these teachings to life. Otherwise they remain empty words, or worse, calcify into religious ideology. And we know how easily religious ideology can be used to justify senseless brutality.

Speaking directly to the Governor, I asked,

> What is a leader? A leader has power, a leader has force at his disposal. It is not wrong to use strength appropriately. But what is true strength? Can one be strong and wise? Strong and compassionate? A force for good?
>
> A wise and strong leader protects his people, inspires them with hope and a vision based on enduring values such as compassion. He is practical and understands in Abrahamic terms that "as ye reap, so shall ye sow," and "by the fruits of your deeds shall ye know thee."

Our actions and intentions create a web of impacts that radiate everywhere for a long, long time, leaving either benefit or suffering in their wake.

In Buddhism, it is not just our actions that matter, but even more so it is the *intention* behind our actions that determines their effects. I have chanted the purification *gatha* (verses) above for fifty years. Recognizing and atoning for the harm we have caused is important. But intention is complex. Freud told us that our motivation is mostly unconscious and we often have simultaneous and contradictory motivations. Purifying our intention for the awakening and healing of all beings is not limited to reciting a gatha, chanting a chant, or practicing and generating benevolence. "The road to hell is paved with good intentions." John Holt would humorously warn educators that "the helping hand strikes again." And recall the Aboriginal elder, "If you have come to liberate me, turn around and go home." Recent leaders such as Dick Cheney and Vladimir Putin were certain their forces would be greeted as liberators. They both claimed, as nearly all invaders do, that they are liberating the long-suffering residents, doing it for their own good. So they take for granted that their intentions are 'beyond reproach.' While Cheney and Putin might have been caught up in ideology and confused as to their real intentions, the Iraqi people understood Cheney's true motives soon enough, as the Ukrainians did Putin's. So we have reason to be skeptical about our intentions.

PSYCHIC FUELS

Let me describe how I came upon an activity I call *tracking the traces of the impacts of our actions* and why I think it is important in the continuing education of the Zen teacher and in activating the Buddhist dream. But first let's explore something more elusive and more catalytic than motivation or even intention, something I call *psychic fuels*. There's a story to it.

I worked for several years with incarcerated teenagers and young adults, supervising graduate students who were providing individual and group mental health services in a variety of settings, from residential camps and jails to community-based schools-within-a-school. I decided to sit in with one supervisee in group therapy sessions, and by the end of the first session, I realized that traditional psychodynamic group process would not work. We needed to be more interactive, more real people than traditional therapists to these adolescents whose lives were in chronic crisis. One day, I asked the group what mattered most to them in their lives. This generated lots of discussion since few adults had ever asked them a question like this with real interest. What really matters, why do you think it matters, how do you know it matters, and how did it come to matter so much? As the students came to trust us, they laid it out: Conquering girls, "bling," lots of money, their "Moms," how many guys they could beat up, hanging with the toughest, coolest dudes, and so on.

Over time, they began to include other things, like making a difference in someone's life, happiness – more altruistic and even existential matters. Then I asked what happened when they acted out of what mattered to them. Initially many scratched their heads but then they dove in. It began to dawn on me that I was asking about motivation, intention, core values, internal working models, and philosophies of living, although I did not use these words. When you are driven by having to have lots of bling and wanting to be the top dog, or belonging to and being taken care of by the top dog, where does that lead you? What are the results? What fuel are you using to power your 'ride,' and what are the effects? Does it burn cleanly, corrosively? We would just discuss these topics, without moral lessons or judgments.

I thought 'psychic fuels,' energies, not simply unconscious wishes and conflicts. What emotional fuel is driving your behavior? What these students valued and held most dear generated certain emotional qualities that drove and informed their behavior and then led to certain results. Mostly, this worked unconsciously – without reflection.

I began to see that we were also discussing the law of cause and effect, karma or action, a central teaching in classical Buddhism but relatively underprivileged in Zen and generally not considered directly at all in psychotherapy. It is not only our outer behaviors but also our inner intentions that determine what unfolds from a certain state of mind, action, or interaction. The impacts from our intentions radiate far and wide in visible and invisible ways that last a long time. But how can we truly determine an intention given that motivations are multiple and unconscious? Two identical actions can exist but one is at the service of awakening and healing and compassion and the other is not. This question – in service to what – became central for me.

I was initially skeptical of practices such as *metta*, or loving kindness meditation, that sought to consciously generate particular beneficent spiritual qualities of mind and heart. My concern was that such practices could potentially obscure a conflicting unconscious inner motivation or affective state. I now think they can be very helpful but are also limited.

These ideas were useful in exploring what gets 'lost in translation' between realization (in which the universal and particular are inextricably interwoven) and personalization (by which we bring to life and apply that realization in the particulars of our daily living).

I began to see that the fuels driving these young women and men were, in turn, determining their fates: scores of their homeboys and homegirls injured or dead, family members caught up in gang violence, pregnancies that brought children they could not care for, fine minds wasted. The cause-and-effect relationships were clear, informed by the notion of psychic fuels (similar but not reducible to unconscious motivation and intention) – energies outside our awareness that inform, drive, and infuse our behavior. What we convey without knowing it. What is transmitted (communicated) through our interactions, no matter what we consciously said, meant, or felt. These generate resonating impacts that ripple across the filaments of Indra's Net and continue reverberating in unpredictable ways for a long time. It was like what Murray Stahl, my freshman psychology teacher, told us about parenting: "It's not what you say but who you are."

This 'who you are' is not a fixed and permanent entity,
but a shifting field of motive forces, if you will.

Let's rewind to the many scandals with Zen teachers; All felt their motives were unimpeachable, they were doing it for the good of the student or the sangha. Often it took real struggle for those affected to say that the abuse happened and that it was harmful, not benevolent. Psychic fuels are conveyed and picked up on and have their impacts through unconscious emotional communication in the relational field, so that often, as in the Stockholm syndrome, the victim takes on the mindset of the abuser.

Indulge me now as I share a personal example so we can see psychic fuels in operation. A series of humbling and illuminating experiences with how my body moved in space became a kind of laboratory for studying and driving home how this operates: an 'up-close and personal' experience of Indra's 'emotional' Net at work. After playing tennis for many years, I began, as a young man with thick inflexible leg muscles to do yoga and approached it ambitiously. The result was an injury to my hip capsule that spawned other joint injuries and early-onset osteoarthritis. For a few years in my late twenties, I could not walk very well, and this was alarming and depressing. Muscle groups throughout my body had compensated for the original injury, and although I exercised, I was stiff, out of balance, and unable to do activities I enjoyed, like playing tennis, because of the resulting inflammation. A side effect was not being able to sit in the lotus or half-lotus position. I consulted with a physical therapist who worked hands-on to mobilize the joint; It was painful. She was reviving a frozen joint, frozen functioning, and it took a while to come to life and for range of motion to improve.

My gait was completely off-kilter, and I needed to learn to walk again. I was banging into things as I wobbled at home. Things would feel more stable, a new normal set in, then more gains and release would prompt another destabilization, and I was again thrown off balance. This cycle continued, but the valleys and troughs evened out, and I came to feel in a new normal kind of body. It passed through my mind how analogous this was to protecting an emotional or psychic wound or trauma. Then things got really interesting.

When I bumped into something, it would hurt, throw off my balance, and things would slide into their old twisted configuration. Suffice it to say that I was highly motivated to look at what was going on. I had a general sense that I was hurling my body and hurtling through space. Perhaps I was defying the effects of injury, acting as if I were that eighteen year-old again, competing in a tennis match. But there was more. As I really slowed down the reel and focused in, I thought I observed a whiff of anger in the movements, something that had completely escaped me. Was I banging into something to feel its presence, like an adolescent might interact with parental limits? The psychodynamics were less intriguing than the quality of energy, the psychic fuel that seemed to be driving the movement. I mustered all the mindfulness I could, but it was hard to catch in action. It was taking place beneath the threshold of awareness – but it was not classically unconscious, that is, repressed or split off. It was like trying to catch a daydream or a reverie in the twilight area between waking and dozing off.

I came to notice that anger was occasionally driving my body movements. It was as if I were using my body to emphatically punctuate a just-beneath-the-radar inner dialogue with a 'humph' kind of movement, in which a foot would hit the table leg or my shoulder an open door. At other times, I realized I was in the midst of a movement, say toward the stove, and would pivot in midstream toward the refrigerator, leaving muscle groups going in two directions at once, throwing things out of whack. Economy of movement and mindfulness in motion became the order of the day.

Each action was driven by and had the operational quality and effect of a particular psychic fuel. This fuel engendered impacts that indeed radiated far and wide and for a long time, in my body, in ways I did

not like, and that motivated me, as suffering is wont to do, to have a closer look. I learned that something I thought was completely outside the realm of my control could be influenced by mobilizing, not only my joints, but also my attention, and in ways I hadn't exactly learned to do on the cushion, or learning to be a therapist. To a Zen student in the sudden-awakening tradition, this was a gradual awakening of great importance to my well-being. It was like Paul Ekman discovering micro-emotions, but here they were at play in physical movement. All this arose in conjunction with the unearthing of a hidden self-concept.

It dawned on me at the time that I was not caring for my best emotional interests very well, and there might be something of a closet samurai in me. This was new information since I had always been quite sensitive to my feelings and the feelings of others. I would often speak of the importance of opening to, rather than shutting down, our emotional life. But, as life events and circumstances revealed another layer of emotional vulnerability, even fragility, and the need to care for and protect my emotional well-being, I realized that I had been a kind of emotional samurai. I prided myself in meeting each thing, event, or feeling 'just as it was,' reflecting of course both the Zen and the psychoanalytic spirit, but simultaneously concealing a lack of acceptance and respect for the real *impacts* of certain qualities and certain emotions. I realized that emotions, psychic fuels, and spiritual qualities *really mattered*.

I came to appreciate what classical Buddhism calls the afflictive and wholesome emotions and their impacts. As a young Zen student, I recall my teacher saying that when we were not feeling compassionate, we should *act* with compassion. This rankled me: Why should I pretend? I had accepted the teaching when tired, sleep; when hungry, eat; when feeling anything, just feel it, meet it head-on. But, I had unconsciously put this teaching – however well internalized and expressed in the Zen training setting – in service to something else. It had become a banner behind which I remained unaware of the impacts of some emotional events, occasionally self-generated.

An annoying arrhythmia was another teacher about the interplay among thoughts, feelings, and soma and the powerful impact of primary emotional states. At first, a physician told me there was no emotional contribution, but I knew there must be, because factors were at play at the time that were heartbreaking and outside my control, and I was feeling both despairing and helpless. Over the years, I have become more able to track powerful, emergent emotional states and the initial rumblings, the precursors of the arrhythmia.

The hallmark of trauma is a strangled scream, a suffocated sob, something like Munch's painting by the same name. For several years, I have provided support for an event honoring parents whose children were killed in Iraq and Afghanistan. Witnessing a hundred tables on which parents lovingly placed their child's things, vivid expressions of his or her whole life, evoked such a feeling. One evening, I awoke with such a powerful emergent sob, fueled this time by an old trauma, the loss of my father, coming to life again. When the arrhythmia kicked in, I made the connection. Since then, a new surgery and, who knows, perhaps this kind of deepening self-observation have contributed to the arrhythmia abating.

The double helix of spiritual and emotional growth, *and* of conscious and nonnconscious experience and practice – a kind of binocular vision – seemed like an apt working metaphor for a Zen guy integrating what we can call the whole self.

CONTINUING EDUCATION

Many in Buddhism focus on seeing things as they 'really are.' But perhaps our perceptions, on the one hand, and 'what is,' on the other, co-arise? What if our perceptions themselves are infused and informed by a guiding myth, a dream. What if we awakened to 'what is' as we perceive and create it? In Zen, no matter our kensho, no matter the 'transmission outside of words and letters,' no matter our presentation of koans, the proof of the pudding is in the eating. How does insight manifest? What are we actually conveying? How is it cultivated and expressed in action? Some may counter, "These are dualistic categories; it is one movement, not 'even one.'" Since words can be put at the service of different functions, this may be so, and it may also be so much hot air. We need to track the fruits, understand that they often differ from what we assume, realize that it takes other skills to do this tracking, and keep learning.

In accord with understanding, psychic fuels, energies, spiritual qualities, are we connecting the dots, making links, deriving meanings, acting on them, perceiving? Aitken Roshi says that we live Buddha's dream; I'm adding that we create it moment to moment. It is the same with the psychotherapeutic dream of fully welcoming the disparate and disowned parts and experiences, making space for them as we widen our tent of the self, the space of the heart. Dylan sings: "I'll let you be in my dream if I can be in yours." We each are by nature in one another's dream, moment to moment dreaming one another. It behooves us to cultivate a mutually beneficial dream.

Currently, many say, "It's just your story, let it go." But it is our story, our dream – what drives us, what we live and stand by, what actually gets communicated in our moment-to-moment interactions, no matter what our conscious intention. How we connect the dots – that makes all the difference in the world. This story is not ego aggrandizement; it is what we live by, how we live, and what we leave in our wake.

Recall the baseball metaphor of the five-tool player: He can hit for average, hit for power, throw, field, and run. In Buddhist practice, some have deep insight, some highly focused *zazen*, some study and follow the precepts closely, endeavoring to embody them. From this aligned alchemy arise wisdom and compassion, in action. Can we be Buddhist and be five-tool players? Not perfect, mind you, but can we develop and integrate dhyana, prajna, and sila well-enough so that they are in alignment and naturally potentiate one another?

Yasutani Roshi's poem conveys the experience of what I take liberties in calling the Bliss Body,

> Vividly clear, vividly clear, manifesting itself.
> The mountains, river, the great earth, the uncovered source.
> There are the flowers, there is the moon – who is the Master!
> Spring, Autumn, Winter and Summer compete with new garb.[10]

This conveys the direct experience of insight into our essential nature and that of all beings (prajna). Then there is strong attentional practice on the cushion (dhyana), turning toward truth, opening, not just to the pure suchness of the birds and clouds, but to what comes forward from unconscious emotional communication, from intimate and other relationships. We continue to refine the jewel, both through zazen and koans that sharpen the enlightened eye (prajna) and by refining our personal and interpersonal being-in-the-world. When we ask, "In service to what?" and "How and to what ends am I using the treasure?" we are acknowledging that we don't know, and we are open to using data from interactions and relationships to shine a ray of darkness into the matter. We consult not only with the unconscious impacts of our actions and the psychic fuels they convey, data that can sometimes be available in somatic experience, but we also check in with our pets, our intimates, and track *après coup* the fruits, the traces we have left in our wake. Sila – enlightened activity, ethical conduct, goodness, mutual benefit – is both a result and an engine of this activity. Wisdom and compassion drop away conceptually as they wed experientially.

Zen master Dogen wrote:

> To be enlightened by the 10,000 things is to free one's body
>   and mind
> and those of others.
> No trace remains
> and this traceless enlightenment is continued forever.[11]

Do not suppose that this amounts to riding off into the sunset in per-petual liberation. This "no-trace that is continued forever" needs main-tenance and refinement. There is a risk that these qualities and their alignment can calcify and lull us into thinking "we're there" and there is literally nothing to do. Is genuine curiosity and learning by experience operating? Or, has realization become a stale, lifeless artifact? Suzuki Roshi once responded to a questioner, "Yes, we are perfect just as we are. And we all can use a little improvement."

Recall the Dalai Lama's response and how astute and yet limited it was. A much less innocent example would be the United States' invasion of Iraq. It was for all the 'right reasons': to prevent the spread of nuclear weapons and to install a better government for the Iraqi people. But the way it turned out was quite different; it revealed other elements of the actual motivations: pure greed, and power. These very toxic motiva-tions and energies, these toxic fuels are what determine the outcomes. This is in accord with the Buddhist teaching of cause and effect, but it allows for the fact that there are elements of our impacts we need other means to become aware of in order to be able to refine, to do the work of perfecting our character. There are two elements to that. One is we need community. We can't do it ourselves because we have blind spots. Blind spots are built in! They're not just a function of not good enough practice, or deep enough insight, or misunderstanding the precepts, they "arise endlessly." For every light, there is a shadow. So we need to develop the ability to tune in to what I call the unconscious emotional field, or what the psychoanalyst Adam Phillips called "the black market of emotions."

The continuing education of both the Zen and spiritual practitioner and teacher should ideally include the kind of tracking the impacts that I am describing, which requires an understanding and appreciation of unconscious emotional communication in the relational field. The symbiosis of the bliss body and the unconscious operates only as it is activated and expressed moment-to-moment. Since the universal and the particular inter-are, opening to the unconscious relational field of emotions enriches our enlightened eye, makes us more discerning, and helps bring us into alignment. It opens the gate of wisdom, for right conduct is the living expression of emptiness, in accord with our insight into our fundamental insubstantial and intimately interconnected true nature.

Although many rightfully emphasize the 'mind training' element of Buddhist meditation, our practice is not just a technique, a means to an end – it expresses the universe, and it calls it into being. A true person of no rank is responsible for her impacts in the world, intentional and unintentional. At the end of the film *Black Orpheus* (1959; directed by Camus), two young boys call up the sun with their guitar playing. Like them, we are bringing forth the universe in every act, every perception. Is this myth, or is it realty? Can we trust that what we call up, name, perceive, and thereby bring forward into the universe will be of benefit to all, including ourselves? Nyogen Senzaki (1973), who we heard from earlier, has left us words of instruction:

> Trust your own head
> Do not put on any false heads above your own
> Then moment after moment follow your steps closely
> These are my last words to you.

A true person of no rank responds freely, in accord with circumstances, unfettered, not sticking to concepts such as gain and loss, enlightened and deluded, subject and object. Her actions do not come from a formula, a cookie cutter, and they may therefore seem paradoxical, even contradictory. But this spontaneity ideally is not random or chaotic but infused with prajna – thoroughgoing, internalized understanding of our empty (not a fixed or permanent entity) and interconnected nature – and it responds in accord with the situation at hand. This wisdom must be lived and personalized in the crucible of daily relational living, through practice, or dhyana.

How is Zen 'the perfection of character'? The Bliss Body is a direct, unmediated experience, part and parcel of a narrative of liberation. From the beginning, things just as they are – standing up, sitting down, laughing, weeping – nothing is missing and nothing is left over. How does this penetrate into our everyday conduct, our relationships? The upwelling of compassion that comes with realization wanes as we immerse in everyday life. Continued clarification of enlightenment through koan study and mindfulness in everyday moments helps. But mindfulness needs to be complemented, not only by awareness of emotional and social intelligence or by new ways of thinking about trauma in the body but also by unconscious emotional communication in the relational field, awareness of how we are using our experience, what 'fuel' we are utilizing and conveying, and what unconscious rippling impacts we are generating.

The process of purification of intention, or character, refining the 'agent of compassion,' can stand to benefit from awareness of unconscious emotional communication in the relational field. The person of no-rank trusts his or her own mind, head, heart, and realization. But we need to 'trust and verify.' Why? Because unconscious experience happens, and all of us are, as Sylvia Boorstein says, "just a moment away from a meltdown," from delusion.

As these understandings and practices become more integrated within us and in our behavior, imagine a new normal develops. We observe how things work, the impacts of our actions – inner and outer, conscious and unconscious – on our own and others' well-being. If we are 'turning toward truth,' we learn from experience. There is another question that can arise: How much 'truth' can we take? It is one thing, in circumscribed settings such as the consulting room or the dojo or the dokusan room, to feel 'together,' to welcome all manner of experience in a more accepting way, and to act in an integrated manner. It is quite another to come face-to-face with ourselves and our impacts in daily relational living in real time, or *après coup*. Sometimes it's more than we can handle. But this capacity can grow, and with it we can have many moment-to-moment awakenings to what *is* really happening. 'Just-this' moments characterized by deep suffering require contact with something that is 'not suffering' in order to metabolize the pain and awaken to the moment's immanence. A modicum of safety is both needed and generated by this process. The Bliss Body is not always blissful. It has no permanent absolute substance and cannot be bought or sold. It is not respectable, and has no meaning and no particular 'use.' Yet, its 'marvelous functioning' – eating, sleeping, falling down, getting up, laughing, weeping, grieving, rejoicing, being born, dying – never ceases.

We open ourselves to learning from the depths – now the universal, now the particularly personal. There are moments when both dissolve, others when they interpenetrate. We cultivate openness to the impacts of living. Psychoanalyst Neville Symington offers a vivid image for psychic suffering. He says that character organizes around the "bee-stings" of relational living. They hurt; it is pointless to pretend that they feel good. The capacity and the ongoing willingness to bear and transform them is crucial. This is the 'standing' we spoke about that co-arises with understanding.

With the ever-renewing new normal – physical, emotional, and spiritual – we become more at ease, less subject to insults and injuries, more naturally restoring and self-righting. We can 'trust our own heads' (and hearts, minds, and bodies) not only because we follow the precepts, not only because we have internalized a sense of ethics, but also because we are, moment-to-moment, experiencing, tracking, and refining our 'impact in the world' – and feeling the sting as we wake up to things that unsettle and trouble us. We also wake up to the other side: how certain fuels and actions generate mutual benefit in their wake. This entire movement, this entire function requires us to be *multilingual.* The two paths not only contain and hold us as we change, they also restrain and temper us with their respective vernaculars and their disciplines.

We live more freely, peacefully, and ethically, creating in an unforced way more buoyancy, aliveness, and true contentment and less pain and harm for all. As an emotional samurai who prided himself on nondualistically meeting whatever emerges head-on, I once found this hard to accept. But, we practice selectively focused attention (without being Pollyannas and Goody Two-Shoes) so that we 'water' and amplify those tendencies that lead to mutual benefit and restrain ourselves from acting on afflictive psychic fuels, greed, ill-will, and delusion. We stop, look, and listen; reflect on our experience; pick up cues when things are awry and out of alignment; stay open to unconscious emotional communication in the relational field; ask "in service to what?" and become aware of how we are (or are not) "turning toward truth" – until it becomes second nature. Then, we again take a sounding of the entire field and keep "following (the impacts and ripples of) our steps."

In the next chapter we will explore the activity of agents of compassion, persons of no rank. How together we activate Buddha's dream and transform profound traumatic suffering. Dhyana, Prajna, and Sila on the collective dimension are Peace, Freedom, and Justice. When they are aligned and fully functioning, there's the alchemy of healing and awakening, compassion and wise action.

4

AGENTS OF COMPASSION:
THE TRANSFORMATIVE POWER
OF COMMUNITY

In this chapter, we explore the challenges and opportunities of bringing our no-self nature into the local and global commons, fraught as it is with greed, hatred and delusion. We illuminate the subtle, fundamental identity of *self and world* that is revealed, internalized and embodied in Buddhist awakening. As we refine a person of no rank – ungraspable in any final or absolute sense, yet embodied in each of our activities – we simultaneously transform the culture and the world. And as we face and work with transforming sociocultural forces of greed, hatred, and delusion, we create and refine ourselves as agents of compassion.

I describe an original process called *turning ghosts into ancestors* that I uncovered in working with veterans and their family members. As in Buddhist theory and practice, it is not primarily the extent or frequency of traumatic suffering that highjacks our security and well-being but our inability to face, respond to, and transform it. To do this, we need the minds and hearts and presence of others, of the beloved community. I explore examples of how this transformative process, which I name the Eightfold Noble Path to Transforming Trauma, operates, drawing from my work at the Coming Home Project and from the Standing Rock Resistance Camp, which I participated in. I weave in the mobilization of the Sandy Hook/Newtown community of parents, and the Mothers of the Movement, mothers who have lost children to random gun violence.

As dhyana, prajna, and sila come into alignment and generate wise and compassionate intent and responsiveness, the robustly singular true person of no rank (who simultaneously finds intrinsic affinity with all beings) becomes an "agent of compassion." I first heard this expression from Aitken Roshi but didn't realize why I liked it until recently. *Agent* implies a sense of agency, a sense of empowerment, the exercise of response-ability – things can be done. We, like the Buddha, as Buddhas, rise from the meditation cushion and enter the commons, which is fraught with anguish.

I write this book through the eyes of a Zen teacher and psychoanalyst. But my personal and professional trajectory has taken me off the beaten path. For the past four decades, I have been creating nondenominational learning and healing environments that bring together the 'best' of East and West. While a freshman at City College of New York, I worked in recreation programs for disadvantaged youth at East Side House Settlement in the South Bronx, traversed Harlem photographing children, and created after-school enrichment programs for minority youth in the suburbs of Paris. I brought young parents together for tea while their toddlers played and made art in a daycare center in working class London, and founded a cooperative nursery school in culturally diverse rural Hawai'i. While training in Zen Buddhism, my teacher and I led a meditation group for incarcerated adults before mindfulness became popular. Much later I began an educational and support program for high-conflict divorcing families at a large urban medical center, created mentoring and meditation groups for incarcerated teenagers, and residential learning workshops for mental health practitioners on Buddhism and emotional growth. I spent eight years with friends offering integrative retreats for Iraq and Afghanistan service members and veterans, their families and children, and their care providers.

As I look back, the thread that runs through all of these endeavors is a profound conviction of the transformative power of community. I see now that I have been a community activator, helping catalyze the connectedness and healing that lay latent within and among us, waiting to be unleashed.

—⁓—

During the stress of the worst of the COVID pandemic, there was so much upheaval I found myself saying, "It is a revolutionary act to breathe in, and a radical act to breathe out." It later occurred to me that for many, breathing in and out was a great challenge if not impossible. Planting an organic garden to benefit the needs of the local community is also revolutionary. Writing a song expresses the Great Functioning. Loving our children, partners, and parents cannot be taken for granted. The world is us and we are the world. The smallest actions radiate, ripple out in ways we cannot predict. And we are receiving ripples, benevolent and malign, continuously.

But it's also true that there are destructive and toxic *systems* of individuals, institutions that persecute, that leverage and weaponize the powers of greed, hatred and ignorance, especially during calamities and catastrophes, for their own benefit. The fossil fuel industry is one such example. Aitken Roshi used to sit out on the corner in downtown Honolulu and Hilo holding a sign that read, "The system stinks." But who creates systems? People do. And what poisons people and other living beings and their habitats? Systems. We can debate this conundrum and ask what is a right response during these times. As we saw in Bernie Glassman Roshi's schema – not-knowing, bearing witness, and compassionate action – engaging the entire process wholeheartedly inclines us toward a benevolent response. I am more interested, however, in how to catalyze a *powerfully aligned* response.

When we personalize the Dharma, we are allowing our idiom to express itself, just as John Coltrane does in his version of *My Favorite Things*. We hear the sounds of suffering and respond according to what we (unconsciously, for the most part) hold most dear. The Quakers call it their inner light. As a Zen guy I found it somehow difficult to call my work with veterans my calling, but over time I came to see that it was. It was determined by many, many factors: idiosyncrasies, proficiencies, lacunae, traumas, wishes, desires, philosophies; I can't name all the factors. They all came together, and the work benefitted many, including me. It emerged slowly but then took on an ineluctable trajectory. I could trust it.

What calls you? What impassions you? For some it's refugees, for others children, yet others rivers and streams and the protection of the more-than-human world. For me, I see that it was the dream of a diverse group of people pulling together in solidarity, standing shoulder-to-shoulder to do the Buddha's work of healing and awakening. If we have eliminated or evacuated or dissociated many good usable elements of our character, perhaps from trauma or perhaps from our idea of what spiritual practice is supposed to be, then we have neither the energy, the staying power, nor the discernment to enter and accomplish the path of 'coming home together action,' an awkward translation for a Japanese word I've forgotten.

About fifteen years ago, I began to feel that "I belong to the world." After decades of working intensively with individuals, I felt "called" to create environments to heal the seen and unseen injuries of war. In the next two sections, I tell part of that story and what we learned together. I share these stories because *all of us*, not just veterans of war or other catastrophic disaster, carry the residues of trauma, personal and collective. What we learned may be of benefit therefore to us all.

Coming Home Part One – Becoming Real

It's January 2007, the opening moments of our first Coming Home Project retreat, an opportunity for veterans and families from around the country to come together to share stories and support one another. We gather for our first circle, thirty-three veterans and family members from seven states, with four facilitators. In the opening moment of silence, as we remember those unable to be with us, Ben, Stefanie and Michael's three-year-old son, is playing with Isaiah, also three, around the edges of our circle. Amid the reverent quiet, we hear Ben say, "My daddy died in Iraq." We learn later from Stephanie that Michael actually committed suicide six months after returning home. Out of the mouths of babes, the first words spoken at a retreat have their own truth: something inside Michael did die in Iraq.

As I reflect on Ben's words, I see the roots of what would blossom over the next six years: in a safe space, short on judgment and filled with compassion, an environment where trust and belonging prevail, veterans and their families would express their truth, their experience of war. Toddler Ben spoke to everyone and we heard him loud and clear. He laid the groundwork for a weekend of truthtelling and a reliable path to healing the traumas of war.

Given the chance, veterans and their families – and all survivors of trauma – want to reconnect and heal. They are looking, unconsciously, for a setting and for conditions in which to do so. We all have this drive, what my dear friend, psychoanalyst Jean Sanville, called reparative intent. For retreat participants, it begins as they come together as fellow veterans, spouses and partners, children and teenagers, parents and grandparents, siblings, uncles and aunties, finding and creating affinity. In an atmosphere of safety it spreads; family members rebuild bridges, and everyone begins to connect with something inside that has gone untended.

Ken Sargent, a Marine master sergeant, and Rory Dunn, an Army specialist, are both Iraq veterans who sustained severe traumatic brain injuries that required life-saving and massive reconstructive surgery. Ken was shot in the head, Rory was hit by an improvised explosive device (IED). Both also suffer from post-traumatic stress. As people mill around, Rory and Ken meet for the first time, up close and personal. Since neither can see very well, they touch each other's wounds, comparing scars and injuries. They are long-lost brothers. The process of making emotional connections palpable has begun.

Rory was angry and bitter. It wasn't just the open head injury that cost him the sight of his left eye and resulted in a brain rebuilt partially with plastic filler. He was also upset about the buddies in his unit who died in the massive IED attack on his twenty-second birthday, and about the associated failures in leadership. "No one but a vet can understand another vet" are his first words. But at the end of the day, he says to a civilian volunteer, "You're alright." As he is leaving, I notice a scrap of paper on the floor near his seat, pick it up, and ask if it's his. He says, "Yeah, it's nothing." I look at it and see a note, with three family trees. I ask him about it: "It's all the people back home blown away by my buddies' dying." I look and see the words: "girlfriend," "baby," "church members," "mother," "father," "sister," and so on – three little stories, three little family trees. Radiating impacts that eat at him. Although Rory sustained a severe traumatic brain injury (TBI) and post-traumatic stress, given the chance, he reclaims not just the piece of paper, but an important part of his emotional life. He is able to leave with a measure of hope and trust.

War trauma, like much cumulative trauma, is like an IED blast. The sonic waves radiate out on multiple levels simultaneously, fragmenting the intrinsic connections within the body, brain, mind, and soul, fragmenting family, social supports, relationships with community, with the institutions and leaders responsible for protection, and with the entire culture. Repairing this pervasive fracturing means regenerating capacities for connectivity at every level, waking up from the dissociative fog of war that enshrouds all the players in this devastating cycle, transforming the traumatic residues, and learning from experience.

Visible injuries, including amputations and disfigurements, were remedied with astonishing medical advances. Not so the unseen wounds, including closed-head mild and moderate traumatic brain injury, post-traumatic stress, and pervasive moral and spiritual injuries, and suicide. Throughout history, warriors have returned bearing visible and unseen scars. But today – after the longest wars in U.S. history – our entire country is shell shocked and benumbed.

Yet many civilians during the Iraq war were interested in communicating with veterans and their families – in both learning from them and sharing with them. Our first weekend workshop was preceded by a community gathering of 250 people at the First Congregational Church in Berkeley. Presenters were military officers, Buddhist teachers, veterans, spouses, and poets. A few attended to see whether a fight would break out among incompatible presenters; it didn't. To the contrary, the diversity made for an inspiring, heartwarming, and heart-wrenching evening. The next day, workshop participants who had been in the audience said they were surprised so many people cared enough to come out to hear what they had gone through. One said he woke up the next morning "with the wind at my back."

The two undeclared but very real wars we endured in Afghanistan and Iraq have fostered a numbing sense of unreality. U.S. media were prohibited from showing the coffins of the fallen arrive back home. Body parts of those killed were discarded or destroyed and not included in burials. We are still coming face-to-face with the costs. And not long after we pulled out of Afghanistan, another brutal was has begun in Ukraine.

A *New York Times* article reported that an attack by American helicopters that left 23 Afghan civilians dead was found to have been a mistake caused by an undigested "swirl of data." The nature of war has changed, with a growing emphasis on "surgical" and tactical strikes and the use of drones. More and more American Air Force pilots go to war by sitting in front of a series of screens, right here in Nevada, New Mexico, and California. Not surprisingly, some service members have great trouble focusing – and even more importantly, some become desensitized and prone to glaze over – a modern variant of the old "thousand-yard stare," a phrase popularized when *Life* magazine published a painting by World War II artist and correspondent Tom Lea portraying a marine at the Battle of Peleliu.

For airmen who operate drones thousands of miles away from their targets, the stress lingers when the shift is over. Anthony, an airman first class, says his "brain hurts each night" when he returns home. He tries working out but what actually helps the tension ebb is "just being able to enjoy a nice bowl of cereal with almond milk." Video games, the activity of choice for many veterans, don't do the trick. "I need something real," Anthony says.

That something real, we learned, is actuated by reconnecting in a safe community of veterans and families. For eight years, my colleagues and I worked with thousands of returning troops and their family members, helping create just such a community. Community grows a connective social tissue where the unseen injuries such as post-traumatic stress and traumatic brain injury can be safely addressed. "Something real" is discovered by coming alive to the beauty in the great outdoors, hiking the Sierras, journaling in a grove of old-growth redwoods, or rafting down a river. It is coming back to one's body, to the present moment, through practices like mindfulness and qigong. It is learning to laugh again with buddies, with partners and children.

Our reintegration retreats created trust, belonging, and camaraderie; veterans came to feel safe enough to open up with one another, and with non-veterans, about experiences they have rarely if ever shared with anyone. As a psychoanalyst (and as a patient), I had experienced the transformative power of the emotional connections that develop in the consulting room. My intuition told me they could be cultivated in a non-psychiatric, community-building group setting characterized by unconditional acceptance. But I did not anticipate being moved to tears in the moments before our first retreat when I saw Kenny and Rory come up to within inches of the other, straining to see, and then spontaneously trace with their fingers the contours of one another's scars. They wanted to make contact, and we were providing the opportunity for them to do just that.

As I mentioned, Jean Sanville called this "reparative intent" and said we all have it. We are wired to connect. She liked to quote child psychiatrist Rene Spitz, "Life begins in dialogue and all psychopathology can be seen as derailment of dialogue." War represents just such an unraveling of natural connections and the capacity to make them. But this ability can be restored, when the right ingredients are present.

⁓⤜

Buddhism has always addressed suffering, but trauma has only recently come into its purview and is not yet a part of its narrative. Here's what we learned about traumatic suffering and how it is transformed (not eliminated).

Coming Home Part Two –
Turning Ghosts into Ancestors

"What's the matter? The war's over," someone said to a veteran. "Yeah," she replied, "over and over and over."

War trauma brings in its wake a collapse of time. The present is engulfed; the past colonizes moment-to-moment experience; and the future is collapsed. Severe Moral Injury and all variants of PTSD are characterized by an experience of haunting. I am not referring to religious 'demons' but rather to unprocessed experiences that have been sequestered away and frozen in time in the interest of survival. Their impacts are potent and fearfully unpredictable and they cannot be easily identified or contained, not to mention explored and transformed.

Ghosts

In mythology, ghosts have no roots, and their restless wandering does not cease – and does not cease to disturb the living – until they are properly honored. Veterans and other trauma survivors can feel as if they are possessed, as if something is clamoring or silently exploding or imploding.

There is a way a ghost becomes an ancestor, and traumatic experiences become memories. The community provides the connective emotional tissue that can hold these otherwise unmetabolizeable experiences. Fear of falling through the cracks abates; we stop holding our breath in traumatic reaction and anticipation, and we finally exhale. We hold ourselves less tightly wrapped and come to trust that we are supported. As trust deepens, we allow ourselves to engage again in the moment. The community provides a container in which unrepresented anguish can be represented, re-experienced in a new key, and transformed from a haunting ghost into a memory, something in the past and no longer omnipresent. The integrative and dynamic process I call turning ghosts into ancestors depends both on consciously cultivated attentiveness and unconscious emotional activity in the relational field.

This transformative activity was named by the psychoanalyst Hans Loewald. Although he was referring not to dissociated traumatic residues such as war generates but to the unconscious byproducts that ensue when we repress sexual and aggressive drives, "Turning Ghosts into Ancestors" speaks directly to the struggles we have been discussing: "Those who know ghosts tell us that they long to be released from their ghost life and led to rest as ancestors. As ancestors, they live forth in the present generation, while as ghosts they are compelled to haunt the present generation with their shadow life."

I want to introduce you to two veterans, Robert and Arnold. Robert was remote and suspicious, and one could palpably feel just how depressed he was. A heavyset Iraq veteran, he came with his wife, who stayed close at all times. But he was not responsive to her, or to anyone for that matter. Arnold had a gruesome tour in Afghanistan, witnessing things he could barely acknowledge. After returning he alternately withdrew and exploded. After blowing up at his son for being "soft," something Arnold of course could never let himself feel, Arnold flew into a rage and shoved his son against the wall. He admitted he'd really felt like killing him. Ashamed, alarmed, and afraid, he fled his own house and did not return. The retreat was the first time he had been in the same room with his son for three months. In the group of fifteen fellow male veterans, he spoke little and often sat with his head near his lap, his face covered. Once, after beginning to speak, he bolted from the room. We'll return later to Robert and Arnold.

Earlier, we met drone pilot Anthony, who said his brain hurt each night after returning home. Working out and video games, activities of choice for many veterans, didn't work for him. "I need something real," he said. This experience of hearts and brains hurting, of "going out of my head," is also represented in a poem by Zen master Thich Nhat Hanh.

For Warmth
I hold my face in my two hands
My hands, hollowed to catch what might fall from within me
Deeper than crying
I am not crying
I hold my face in my two hands
To keep my loneliness warm
To cradle my hunger
Shelter my heart, from the rain and the thunder
Preventing my soul from flying in anger[12]

Writing from his own struggles, Nhat Hanh wrote also for the thousands of his fellow Vietnamese being shattered by destruction and loss during what the Vietnamese call the American War. In the poem, he cradles his head in his two hands to prevent his soul, or his humanity, from fleeing in anger. *The Scream*, a renowned work of Norwegian painter Edvard Munch, captures the agony, the shock, and the helpless despair of severe trauma. The figure in the painting, who seems to both have seen and to be a ghost, has his hands over his ears, blocking out sounds, but could just as well be holding his head, preventing it from exploding with terror, leaving a vacant shell of a man.

Despite the surges of adrenaline and the profound bonding of going through hell together in the war zone, the sense of being real is often a major casualty of war trauma. Paradoxically, dissociation can also protect hidden corners of one's humanity from further damage. Chunks of lived experience retreat into a kind of witness protection program. "Can I get a witness?" becomes more than an old R & B song; it is one of the deepest desires of veterans and their families.

Army wife Angela Ricketts was going through a particularly bad time during one of her husband's many deployments. Her friends advised her to channel her "black soul," a phrase they used to mean going numb. Angela's words for this experience, to "hover above," clearly reflect dissociation, in service of making it through in one piece. Being in multiple pieces paradoxically helped her feel intact. Only when it was likely that her husband would not be deployed again could she "step back and really feel," a precursor to a more durable inner peace than "pieces" can provide. By dissociating potentially overwhelming emotions, Angela stayed psychologically alive until a time when she felt her husband would be reliably there to listen, when they could face things together. I think her appraisal of when that time was had both conscious and unconscious elements, much like participants' appraisals of safety during retreats.

Turning

Bearing witness is not a passive, impersonal affair. The something real that drone pilot Anthony, other service members, and veterans need is kindled by reconnecting in a safe community. This helps make real what has become numb and lifeless by rendering unprocessed traumatic residues digestible – by making use of healing relational conditions to develop the capacities necessary to transform splintered parts into thinkable, feel-able, dream-able and narrate-able experiences and memories.

The five elements that comprise Coming Home retreats are not a new quick fix, but rather are rooted in how humans have, since time immemorial, worked to transform overwhelming trauma. They include sharing stories in a safe environment (healing dialogue), wellness exercises (spiritual practice), expressive arts, being active in the wild (the healing power of nature and beauty), and secular ritual (adapted from reverent religious experience). The veterans, family members, and providers we have worked with uniformly do not want their own suffering and the suffering of those they hold dear to have been in vain. They want it to mean something. "What have we got to show for it?" one service member asked about a certain campaign. He'd make any sacrifice, including the ultimate one, for a mission that to him made sense. Driven by the reparative instinct and the need for meaning, veterans commonly endeavor to 'make something' of war-related trauma, to 'redeem' it.

What we cannot acknowledge we cannot process. What we cannot process, we cannot transform. What we cannot transform haunts us.

It takes other minds and hearts to help us heal our own, to help us grow the capacities we need to transform suffering. This is done in concert, reweaving the web of connective emotional, relational, and spiritual tissue that cumulative trauma tears asunder. Within an informed, responsive culture, it is possible to transform ghosts into ancestors, to make what haunts us into elements we can hold and properly remember. This opens up the present once again, and the future as well.

Our retreats provided optimal conditions for processing war trauma in a relational field bigger than ourselves, in the presence of others, breathing, listening, witnessing, and sharing our humanity with us. Transforming trauma asks that we recreate and reauthor it, rather than solely experience it as lodged within, a kind of foreign invasive element, inflicted on us, inscribed and burned into our neural and relational circuitry by the profound helplessness to change it. Without working it over and making it our own, overwhelming trauma remains a ghost, what some experience as an 'inner demon.'

A ghost gradually becomes an ancestor, and traumatic experiences become memories, by a most human alchemy. The community holds us as trust grows, and we learn to return our attentiveness to body, breath, peers, family, and surroundings. It provides the buoyancy that genuinely lifts all boats. The military chaplain who we met earlier said that on the final day at a retreat he was able "to exhale" for the first time in three years of working continuously in a large military receiving hospital. In an unconditionally accepting environment, veterans come to feel they belong, feel understood, and become less on the defensive and more open. Wellness practices that reconnect them to ignored and undeveloped inner resources can become internalized. Optimal environments for connecting and healing are also optimal for learning and relearning.

When the environmental conditions are right, participants feel safe enough to represent their experience. In Coming Home retreats this happened spontaneously among peers and family members, in small support groups, and through expressive arts. The fear of shame, humiliation, and other crushing reactions is disconfirmed and replaced by a loving response. Buoyed, they are freer to venture in and share, according to their own rhythm. The content and pacing of what they reveal is at the direction of the participant, modulated according to his or her degree of felt safety so that rarely, if ever, does it re-traumatize. They are supported, as they are ready, in re-experiencing their anguish in a new key.

On the third evening of the retreat, Robert, the heavy-set, profoundly depressed Iraq vet we met earlier, watched a film on grief, one of several programs offered. Two-thirds of the way in, I saw him begin to emerge from his deep freeze. First his eyes began to water, then a few tears ran down his cheeks. When the film ended, he stood up. The color had returned to his face. His arm was around his wife. A few more tears trickled down. He made no effort to conceal or wipe them away. As we approached through the crowd, he began to talk in a low voice about his losses during the war, how unbearable they had been, how he hadn't told anyone. There were more hugs with his wife, conversation, and, during the large group gathering the next morning, he leaned over and gave her a kiss. Everyone took this in.

He began talking with his fellow vets. He was alive again. In a men's veterans group, he described how desperate he'd felt and revealed for the first time how he had tried unsuccessfully to kill himself. During the large closing circle, he surprised everyone by actually speaking and expressing genuine gratitude to all gathered. It was visible that the numbing freeze had thawed, at least for the moment. He seemed to have come back from the dead. Then he said something that stopped me: he looked forward to seeing everyone again next year, if he was still here.

After the retreat, a fellow spouse his wife had befriended contacted us to say that Robert's house was being foreclosed on. This had brought him spiraling back down, and he'd become suicidal. The support and resources he and his wife received from fellow vets and spouses they had connected with at the retreat rallied and helped him make it through the crisis and regain a measure of his aliveness.

Not only is this a huge relief, but repeated instances of this benevolent cycle regrow our capacity to encounter and integrate the 'ghosts.' The power of community support and the inner capacities developed and practiced in this optimal relational setting work in concert to animate and bolster us through this process. Gradually the fear of being retraumatized abates and the traumatic shards reintegrate and take their place as memories. Our sense of meaning becomes renewed. Traumatic experiences thus represented (given form, expressed) and reexperienced, gradually become re-encoded into a transformed, more cohesive worldview. Although painful, they are now memories rather than haunting ghosts. And as they recede to the background, we can paradoxically remember them, think about them, and dream them. They trigger us less because they've become more integrated, and when they do rear their heads, the community and our wellness practices are available to help us meet the surging tides of powerful emotion. We accept ourselves and our broken elements more, we breathe into, rather than react to, the pain, and tame and regulate it better. Not perfectly – the wounds of war do not disappear – but we go forward with reduced anguish, increased hope, aliveness, emotional stability, and connectedness.

Safety, trust, and belonging are the alpha and omega and grow throughout this process. Let's expand the series of R words at play to unpack a sequence that, although operationally more interconnected than strictly sequential, we have seen repeated scores of times. Regulate, recognize, risk, represent, re-experience, re-contextualize (re-integrate), re-encode, and re-author is not a conscious process. It occurs in varying sequences, each element supporting the others, as it is 'practiced' in retreat and off-campus settings. I call these the Eightfold Noble Path to Transforming Trauma.

It begins with the community invisibly helping *regulate affect*, as well as arousal and energy levels, in a *relationally attuned field*. Veterans *recognize themselves* in one anothers' stories, with a resulting destigmatizing and normalizing effect, and in turn *feel recognized*. They become more able to manage the anxieties of becoming visible and to *risk sharing* their story. As they *represent their experience* through expressive arts or verbally in a large or small group or one-to-one setting, they *re-experience* traumatic events that had been haunting them, but in a new setting, where fears of falling to pieces, leaving themselves open to physical harm, being painfully shamed, rejected, and ostracized are disconfirmed by the unconditionally loving *response of the community*. Through *repeated mini-cycles* of this process, traumatic experience is held in a new key.

Turning ghosts into ancestors is a remarkably robust and consistent process, given the right ingredients, and its impacts are reliable and predictable. It enhances post-traumatic growth *whether or not* specific symptoms of PTSD are altered. Stigma was reduced and participants reported highly significant reductions in stress, exhaustion, burnout, anxiety, isolation, hopelessness, and emotional numbness. Further, they reported significant increases in happiness, relaxation, energy, sense of support, and ability to care for and calm themselves. In follow-up studies four to eight weeks out, these positive results remained strongly significant, consistent, and reliable.

Recall Arnold, the vet we met earlier who had blown up at his son and bolted from the family home for three months. After three days on retreat, Arnold felt safe enough to describe how ashamed he was feeling for what he had done. The warm response of comrades-in-arms melted his heart and he cried for a long time. On the final morning of the retreat, with eighty-five veterans and family members sitting in a large circle, participants shared their experience of being together and said their good-byes. After such profound alienation from his family, Arnold approached his shy son and hugged him, bringing both tears and cheers from the group. The pain of isolation had receded, replaced by the warmth and unconditional acceptance of a healing community. Reconciliation takes many forms.

An optimal environment for connecting, transforming trauma, and learning helps regenerate four qualities that distilled out across many retreats: aliveness, bonding, emotional regulation, and finding meaning. Participants attended because the retreats were "not therapy," but they stayed and benefited because the retreats were therapeutic and rebuilt eroded trust, alleviated isolation, and engendered feelings of belonging and being understood.

Reconnection takes patience. Veterans and family members test the waters to see how real and deep they are before venturing in; they want to be sure the environment is genuine and the staff is devoted and skilled. Suspicion runs deep and is wise – adaptive – when you've spent fifteen months in a setting where, as many veterans recount, "people are trying to kill you." No one wants to be retraumatized. At the end of a particularly moving closing circle, there was a silence. I waited, remembering that a voice would often pipe up just when I thought the group was talked out. As I was about to draw things to a close, a woman veteran cleared her throat and began, half in jest, "So when are you guys gonna break out the Kool-Aid?" The entire room cracked up, aware of the residual skepticism.

Let's review: war trauma, like most severe cumulative trauma, is like the shockwaves of an IED, splintering connections on multiple levels and disabling intrinsic capacities to process the trauma itself. An unconditionally accepting and compassionate culture (environment, community, relationship) is the engine for a process of transformation that promotes a repair of these capacities and a transformation (not elimination) of the trauma reflected in what we call post-traumatic growth.

In the Buddhist World

These dynamics apply to many trauma survivors, including Buddhist practitioners who are not veterans or victims of abuse or unspeakable tragedy. An old friend, for example, who's an experienced Zen hand, once told me that he had felt for years that he had to extrude everything that could be called self or personal in order to practice properly. He meant not just letting go of self-referential thoughts during zazen, but evacuating entire parts, whole-scale characteristics of himself that he believed would interfere with his practice.

If, at one pole there's the experience of being *full of self* – self-dealing, self-referential, self-obsessing, and self-aggrandizing – at the other pole, there's my friend, and many, many others who think they must become literally empty of self. They become 'pretend selfless' – with no feelings, thoughts, concerns, desires, and so on. They're in the dojo, the dokusan room, the consulting room, and the general population. Such people are paralyzed, pouring themselves into an inhuman mold, afraid of their emotional life, unable to face, bear, accept and transform their emotional suffering. They are passive, isolated, and sometimes fall apart.

A long-time practitioner in another Zen lineage told me how he sat for years in the zendo, in perfect posture for days upon days, only later to see that he had been "deconstructing his carburetor," and nearing a breakdown. They don't see the possibility of a lotus growing in the mud, of 'flaws' or 'defects' becoming energy to use, even qualities. They can't contribute their gifts to the sangha because they've become impoverished, having offloaded so much of what makes them distinct. Letting go of self, forgetting self is taken *literally*, not a matter of releasing fixed structures, conscious and unconscious attachments to affliction and harmfulness, but as a search and destroy (or erase) mission. Another friend, a long-time Buddhist practitioner, told me it took more than a decade of psychotherapy to discover that the appearance of equanimity for which he was respected in the dojo was actually a form of dissociation or shutting down.

Opening Up

Returning to our Coming Home retreat, five minutes before the end of the final small group meeting of the four-day retreat, a woman who until this moment had been supportive of others but mum about herself was no longer able to hold things back. She described with a flood of emotion how she was sexually assaulted by her commanding officer. We all remained past the time allotted, even though the large closing circle was convening and return flight time margins were tight. During a pause in her account, the group went to finish packing and a facilitator remained with her for the next hour to help her work through and consolidate all that had emerged and discuss strategies for addressing it going forward.

I think three elements contributed to this veteran's decision to risk disclosing this rape for the very first time. One was the lack of coercion; since she knew nobody was going to "make her talk" or "force it out of her," and she didn't want to return home without having herself taken advantage of the opportunity. Two was the fact that we spoke about her in our facilitator meetings, felt that she might need additional support, and one of us volunteered to connect with her over some meals. Three was the silently growing inner sense that she had the emotional hardiness to withstand the impacts sharing this experience would surely bring. This had been cultivated not only by practices like qigong and meditation; it had also been buoyed by having quietly internalized the examples of her sister veterans. Not only did she (mostly unconsciously) conclude that her immediate cultural environment, her sister veterans and the staff, would not harm, reject, or punish her, but she also discovered that her 'processing power' (her emotional or meditative muscle) was strong enough to venture forth.

This experience stirred up tremendous emotional turmoil for this

veteran that needed further attention. But she also felt more peaceful. Dissociated pieces afford us a transitional resting place that can temporarily ensure our physical and psychological survival. But genuine peace only emerges as pieces reconnect.

Most of us know that things are interconnected, but how quickly we forget. The song *Dry Bones* contains the famous lyrics: "The ankle bone connected to the shin bone, The shin bone connected to the knee bone, The knee bone connected to the thigh bone, The thigh bone connected to the hip bone, the hip bone connected to the back bone, The back bone connected to the shoulder bone, The shoulder bone connected to the neck bone, The neck bone connected to the head bone." Then comes a line I had forgotten: "Dem bones, dem bones gonna walk around."

A real person – a true self – emerges as ghosts become ancestors and take their places in a pantheon of diverse memories. This person comes back to life as she inhabits and shapes the present and aspires to a future.

CONNECTING IN THE MIDST OF THE UNSPEAKABLE

The process of forming community to address trauma is instinctual, if allowed to unfold. On December 14, 2012, I watched scenes from the tragic shootings at Sandy Hook School in Newtown, Connecticut. I saw people hugging, comforting, and supporting one another. Connecting. We witnessed the sudden shock and the utter helplessness. The searing loss of loved ones and of meaning. And then people came together again, at the interfaith ceremony. Not to meet the President, they said, but to support one another and feel the comfort of one another's presence.

The impacts of traumatic loss were evident – glazing over, shock, numbness, disbelief, utter helplessness, and despair. People were literally blown away. But they made use of every shred that remained of their responsive capacity to connect with one another, within themselves, and with something greater than themselves. They created spaces, small and large, where they could come together to regenerate safety, trust, and hope, safe environments where their traumas could be represented (given shape and form). Not forgotten or eliminated but transformed from haunting and disabling traumatic residues into memories we can think about and integrate.

Without conscious effort, residents were repairing the pervasive fracturing and regenerating compromised capacities for connection. Unable to fully process or understand, they helped one another stand the trauma, stay awake, and stave off the dissociative fog that ensues after such shocking, unspeakable loss and horror. The community held in trusteeship, as it were, emotions too overwhelming for them to yet explore. This was the heart's natural intelligence at work.

BEARING THE FULL FORCE OF OUR ANGUISH: LEARNING FROM GRIEVING MOTHERS

Safety. Belonging. Unconditional acceptance, without judgment. Attentive listening. Speaking from the heart. Mutual respect. These are the ingredients that make bearing the unbearable possible. These are the elements of a healing environment in which survivors can transform the traumas of war. Those suffering from post-traumatic stress want nothing more than conditions in which they can allow the traumas to resurface and be held and transformed. We have learned that at the heart of such an environment is community: robust, vigorous, and supple. Accepting and loving, a secular version of what church should be like, community is the social tissue that restores, repairs, and regenerates the ruptured connections trauma leaves in its wake within individuals, families, communities, organizations, policy makers, and leaders.

What blinds us to the healing power of community? Is it our individualistic culture? How we seem to thrive on creating invidious divisions? Waiting for the silver bullet that will cure all ills? Blind faith in supposedly helping institutions? All of the above? The absence of community is at the root of many of our social and cultural problems. To review: trauma *shatters* lives and connections, like an IED blast. The erosion of community is the alpha and omega of trauma; its repair requires reestablishing those connections and the communitas they facilitate.

"To sit at a table...and bear the full force of our anguish."
– Lucia McBath, Mothers of the Movement

Lucia McBath nails it. This is a crucial element in transforming overwhelming trauma. Mothers of the Movement is a group of women who have lost children to gun violence and police violence. She said this at the 2016 Democratic Convention talking about her son Jordan Davis. Hilary Clinton provided a healing setting for these grieving mothers. President Obama was skilled at providing such a compassionate, containing presence. His talk after the Newtown massacre is a case in point.

"I am mindful that words cannot match the depth of your sorrow, nor can they heal your wounded hearts. You're not alone in your grief. Know that our world too has been torn apart, that we have wept with you. Whatever portion of sadness we can share with you to ease this heavy load, we will gladly bear it." Speaking of the teachers at Sandy Hook, he said, "You held at bay your shock and trauma because others needed you." He recalled watching "scenes of children helping one another, holding one another." "In the face of unconscionable evil, you looked out for one another, cared for and loved one another." Similarly, President Obama's rendering of *Amazing Grace* at the Charlotte funeral captured the unspeakable pain and seemed to provide a vehicle for binding it and turning it around.

RESISTANCE REPORTAGE:
THE BEATING HEART OF STANDING ROCK –
WALKING THE GREAT MYSTERY WITH ALL MY RELATIONS

How does a people simply endure when they are being wiped out and their survival as a people is threatened? Not passively. We need to be communities of resistance, resilience and healing. In 2016 I had the honor of spending a week in North Dakota, at the Standing Rock Resistance Camp. I witnessed and participated in a remarkable display of peaceful non-violent resistance, fueled by a community that regulated and transformed its trauma, so it could stay buoyant, peaceful, joyful, and in the fight.

From April 2016 to February 2017, tens of thousands of people journeyed to Oceti Sakowin, Seven Fires Camp, in Cannonball, North Dakota in support of the water protectors on the Standing Rock Sioux reservation, in a momentous gathering of tribes, their allies, and people from all walks of life and all ages, standing in solidarity to put a halt to the Dakota Access Pipeline (DAPL) and protect the water of 17 million people living downstream. I took part in an action by 524 clergy on November 3, 2016. At Standing Rock multifaith spiritually-informed direct action was the interplay, in a remarkable contemporary context, of the principles of Native spirituality: The Great Mystery (Wakan Tanka, also Great Spirit) and All My Relations (Mitakuye Oyasin).

Although I practice and teach Zen, I occasionally enjoy attending Quaker meeting. For months I had been following the stories of young people and women leading the movement against the pipeline. It struck a chord in me. As a child, I cut my teeth at various peace demonstrations to which my mother would bring me. From 2006-2016, I helped create and shared a profound healing space with thousands of returning veterans and their family members, hundreds of whom worked in law enforcement. I felt honored to know them. Watching on TV the displays of brutality by law enforcement at Standing Rock evoked outrage and grief. It disturbed me to see officers abusing their sacred protective function; inflicting their power on those devoted to protecting the water, the land, and the health and wellbeing of millions.

Occasionally at Quaker meeting I would stand during silent worship, as is custom, and speak my heart. It felt better to share, even as my voice trembled and my eyes welled up. One day in late October, 2016, I got a message from the secretary of the meeting. A member of the Unitarian Universalist congregation wanted to sponsor someone to go to Standing Rock. The meeting asked if I wanted to go.

I had experience with activism and communities, but I was wary of "the helping hand (that) strikes again," the phrase of John Holt. This unseen principle had wreaked havoc worldwide in time immemorial. As a white male, I also recalled the tensions back in The Civil Rights Movement when whites offered to help blacks fight for their rights, so I did some research and discovered that John Floberg, Episcopal pastor with the Standing Rock Sioux tribe for 25 years, had issued a call for clergy from all faiths to come to support and help protect the water protectors. The action was to occur within days. I didn't hesitate. "Yes," I said.

⚶

At the Bismarck Airport, I met my ride, two pre-Rabbinic Hebrew priestesses who were renting a car. Great company they were and navigating geniuses who led us through miles of unlit, mostly unmarked roads. As I began wondering about the early Hebrews' magical powers, they said they'd learned a trick to download GPS directions to use when there's no signal. They dropped me off at St. James Episcopal Church, which Rev. Floberg had made available. I wanted to be at the campground but didn't think there would be sufficient light to set up in the pitch black. Little did I know that, with the massive floodlights trained all night long on the camp by law enforcement and the Dakota Access Pipeline security, there was plenty of light. People at the large one-room church were unpacking and setting up pads on the floor or ingeniously arranging chair beds, while a few were chatting in the adjacent kitchen. I carved out a tiny sleeping space in the kids' play area. I hadn't slept with a large group of people since my early Zen retreat days. Between people arriving all night long and a few prize-winning snorers, I slept little. But I was glad to be among new comrades.

I got up before dawn and soon met Sarah, the one other person not still in a sleeping bag, who asked if I wanted to take a walk. An Episcopal who had driven from her home in Wisconsin, she spent time each year with families at Pine Ridge, an Oglala Lakota reservation in South Dakota. We enjoyed walking under the stars and watching the light rise over the Cannonball River as we shared stories.

I was itching to get to camp. But someone asked for volunteers to help prepare dinner. We began to make ham-and-cheese, turkey, and peanut-butter-and-jelly sandwiches for the evening, when we'd all gather for training at the gym. A few volunteers turned into a team of dozens, and a 'bunch' of sandwiches into thousands. Three hours later we had made enough sandwiches and assembled enough paper bags with chips and fruit for dinner and also for the next day. I got caught up in the sheer enjoyment of working together with laughing comrades. I called it sandwich *samadhi*, a highly advanced spiritual state of active communion.

Mike, a newly appointed Episcopal Bishop for Oregon, drove me up to camp. Native author Louise Erdrich captures the approach: "The hills and buttes of the Missouri breaks are dotted with isolated houses until the sudden appearance of the Oceti Sakowin encampment. The presence of so many people catches at the heart." I got out of Mike's car and stopped to take in the scope and feel the pulsating life. I walked through the main gate and down the road, following the amplified sound of the camp announcer calling for volunteers down by the river. I found the announcer next to the sacred fire. "Relatives, we need you down by the river, there's an action in progress. If you can witness, that would be great." "Relatives" – that greeting would stay with me as I experienced that he and other Natives meant it. We were in this together.

I set off to find the river. People were going in different directions. There was a group of excited young Lutherans eager to put their bodies where their beliefs were. Someone who seemed like an organizer told us that if we were willing to be arrested or even if we just wanted to witness, we should go register with the Red Owl Legal Collective up on the hill.

I listened to the legal counselors but decided I did not want to be in jail when our clergy action was taking place the next day. Things were fluid, news was continuously breaking, accounts being updated, versions changing by the minute. Waves of information and energy pulsed through camp. There had been a tragedy by the river. Later, there was another casualty: an elder had been hurt. Women and children were now asked to stay back. Then allies too. Something had happened or was happening but it was hard to know precisely what.

I dropped off some warm clothing that friends had sent along and decided to stop and just take things in, sitting down a short distance from the sacred fire in the shade of a few tarps. The swirl of information, activity, and concern quieted down. I sensed a lull, a low kind of feeling. It was as if there were a palpable collective pulse.

A female elder took the mic. As she spoke, I realized anew how we are all one interacting mind, "Relatives, you might think things here are disorganized, even chaotic. But it's an ordered disorganization. We Indians don't put things in squares and compartments. We see circles, we follow intuition. But things get done, they unfold." And how!

She passed the mic to the announcer, who paused. "There hasn't been much going so well the past couple days," he said. Just days before, over 100 water protectors had been arrested and many brutalized. "I think we need some humor. Anyone got any jokes?" When no one came forward, he said, "You know there's such a thing as Native humor. I hope you white folks aren't offended." And he told a series of five or six stories, each funny and with complex, interweaving themes. If inclusion – embracing differences within unity was the order of the day, and it was – things were also pretty nuanced.

"So back in the day, some white folks came to the rez and said 'Where did you Indians get all this money?' They had seen a shiny new USDA building and a few new stores. An Indian said, 'Well, I'll tell you. There was this guy, his last name was Custer. One of the Indians knew him. During a conversation, we learned what he was planning. So we sent a runner over the hills into the city. And we took out a life insurance policy on Mr. Custer.'"

The others gathered didn't show much, but I nearly burst out in laughter. It was a barb for sure, but it was complex. The final joke was short. Someone called out Donald Trump's name. "Nah," said the announcer. "Nah." Another called out, "Come on," but he said, "Nah, he's not worth it." Finally the announcer agreed, "Okay...Okay...Donald

Trump, you're lucky." We waited expectantly, like with a knock-knock joke. "You are lucky, Donald Trump, that you wear a hairpiece." It took a moment but this time I broke out laughing.

After Grandma's words and the announcer's jokes, there was another lull; the down feeling seemed to return. As I made my way toward the main camp road, I passed a young woman carrying a sign that said "Mental Health" and asked her if I could learn more. She showed me where the teepee was and invited me to come by.

Just then a buzz went up, slowly building to a roar, then a cheer. I looked along the road that bordered the sacred fire, and a caravan was rolling up, as if responding to prayers unspoken. On horseback and in pick-up trucks came young warriors, many wearing feathers. They looked like they'd been through an ordeal and carried prayer flags on long poles and a drum. Something was happening, something spontaneous and not measurable in "compartments and squares."

A few Natives formed a circle at the sacred fire and began drumming and singing. The energy of ceremony rose in a sharp dramatic way. From the far corners of the camp, residents began to arrive, drawn by the music, which was surely prayer. Young warriors began to dance, circling the drummers. Elders would touch and bless them. The rising tide of energy was palpable and irresistible. Eyes brightened, we became immersed, and the sense of emptiness lifted as we were carried into the ancient ritual.

The drumming and singing and praying built to a fever pitch, and just when you thought it was over, it would begin again. The crowd had grown to hundreds. The community was revitalizing itself using its ceremonial resources. The drumbeats and cries went right through and in – linking, buoying, energizing, awakening. The ancient was alive. Ancestors felt present. While immersed, I also marveled at how the community was spontaneously raising its spirits by raising The Great Spirit (Wakan Taka) through the presence of All My Relations (Mitakuye Oyasin).

Carried along on this great wave, I glanced around and saw that others were, too. The entire community was infused with a pulsating life-giving energy that linked us all. We were breathing and being breathed in a great communal inspiration. When the prayer stopped, there was a long silence. Something had shifted, a 'climate change' of benevolent aliveness.

That night we got to meet all the other clergy and lay people who had come. As we crowded into the Cannonball Gym, it felt like attending a homecoming or a high-school basketball game. We filled the bleachers and poured out onto the floor. Pastor Floberg had hoped for 100 but well more than 500 were present. We dined on sandwiches, chips, apples and beverages, and heard from John, Native elders, and organizers about the history of Standing Rock resistance camps, what our action the following day would consist of, and how to conduct ourselves. The primary message: We would be peaceful, prayerful, non-violent, and lawful.

When Columbus first set foot on Guanahani island in 1492, he performed a ceremony to "take possession" of the land for the king and queen of Spain, acting under the international laws of Western Christendom. This act of "possession" was based on a religious doctrine now known as the Doctrine of Discovery. In 1823, the Christian Doctrine of Discovery was quietly adopted into U.S. law by the Supreme Court in *Johnson v. McIntosh*. Writing for a unanimous court, Chief Justice John Marshall observed that Christian European nations had assumed "ultimate dominion" over the lands of America during the Age of Discovery, and that - upon "discovery" - the Indians had lost "their rights to complete sovereignty, as independent nations," and only retained a right of "occupancy" in their lands. In other words, Indians nations were subject to the ultimate authority of the first nation of Christendom to claim possession of a given region of Indian lands.

The clergy action on November 3, 2016, would be the first public multifaith renunciation of the Doctrine of Discovery in the presence of elders from a wide range of tribes. Reverend Floberg told us in the gym that we were 524 in number, remarkably the same as the number of years since the Doctrine of Discovery was invoked in the Americas. Myth and reality blurred in a felicitous way.

Upon returning to the church, some who'd stayed the previous night got their knickers in a twist when they saw that a large group of newcomers had taken their places. There was enough space for all, and I thought, "How the beat goes on." How bountiful the opportunities for "helping hands" to learn to walk our talk. Two hundred people slept peacefully on the floor at St. James Church that night.

The next morning, I walked in the dawn light with Zen friends across the hills to the town hall where breakfast awaited. Then we shuttled over to the campground. The area around the sacred fire is not large. With elders from the multiple tribes gathered, residents from camp, and the clergy and lay people gathered, it was quite a crowd. On a clear bright morning, Rev. Floberg convened the ceremony with simple, powerful words. Each of the faith leaders spoke briefly, renouncing the Doctrine of Discovery. They presented each of the nine tribal elders with a copy of the Doctrine. John suggested they could place them in the fire if they wished. I couldn't help but notice the look on the elders' faces: "But of course," they seemed to say. One after another, the elders burned the Doctrine of Discovery.

It was momentous. In the same container as the burning doctrines, elders offered sacred tobacco. They began to smudge the clergy and the other elders. We had been instructed to proceed through the gate and up the hill to the front lines, the 1806 Backwater Bridge, for the rest of our ceremony. But we weren't moving and seemed to be dissipating the momentum that had just been created. When I turned around and glanced up the hill, I realized that every person was being individually smudged from a single ceramic container, the same one that contained the burning Doctrines of Discovery and the sacred tobacco offering. My restless eagerness abated; I saw the transforming alchemy and how it had spontaneously arisen.

We all walked up the hill and assembled at the edge of the bridge. In the middle of the bridge were three Native volunteers policing the event. On the other side of the bridge were concrete barricades, a burned-out semi-truck, scores of county and state police, DAPL security, and numerous police and militarized vehicles. We gathered into a big circle, spreading well up the hillside. John began to speak, but the low-tech sound system could not compete with the helicopters buzzing low over the bridge. Some said they were deploying Stingray spy technology to tap cellphones.

After multifaith prayers, John invited us to come up, asking if we were "singers" or "speakers." The first presenter was a vibrant African Methodist Episcopal female cleric in brightly colored robes. She spoke powerfully and incisively, making clear the connections among racial, economic, political and environmental injustice, No DAPL, and Black Lives Matter, and American slaves, and Native Americans. The Associate Bishop of the Episcopal Church of the U.S., also an African-American woman, followed. She jumped in with "Wade in the water, wade in the water children, wade in the water, God's gonna trouble the water." Her voice rose above the helicopters and we all began to move together,

enrapt, joining in song. Of course, Mni Wiconi! Water is Life! The battle cry of the Standing Rock movement. We were all in the water together, and of the water too. Someone from every denomination represented
sang, spoke, or both. Each was moving and distinct.

There were also sounds coming from another action that had developed nearby, at the middle of the bridge. A group of younger water protectors was pushing the limits, surging toward the police and barricades
on the other side. Restrained by the volunteer Native police, their chants
and protests drew a few from our own ranks.

When the singing and speaking finished, we 524 strong began a
slow ceremonial movement in which the circle folds in on itself and
continues round, permitting everyone to come face to face with everyone else. This we did, one by one, seeing and greeting one another.
Like the smudging earlier, this practice was powerful in its own way,
though not as confrontational as the smaller louder counterpoint out
on the bridge.

Standing by the side of the bridge, I noticed two Native women
who'd both spoken, Lyla June and an elder, perhaps her teacher. I'd
heard they were leading a forgiveness march in two days to the Morton
County Police Station. Rather than suffering paralyzing animosity, they
drew from their Native spirituality to practice and offer forgiveness to
those who had harmed the water protectors. Not everyone agreed with
their approach, but I was intrigued and approached to say hello.

Lyla was finishing a conversation with a young Christian man, a
musician who was wearing a few crosses on chains around his neck.
He had just finished singing them a song, perhaps a song of healing.
He took off a chain and gave it to her. I couldn't see what the amulet
was. I thought it was a cross but later saw it was a purple stone. Lyla
began to weep, then sob. Finally she said, "Oh, your [Christian] 'way'
must have major powers, major spirit…" I thought, A gift? A true gift
from a Christian, a group that has so harmed our people? I think what
might have moved her was the experience of safety and generosity from
someone toward whom she still probably felt suspicious and aggrieved.

As the actions wound down, I walked out to the middle of the bridge
to one of the Native volunteer police. I'd overheard part of his conversation with a water protector and said, "As a veteran, it must not feel so
good to have high powered [sniper] rifles trained on you." He replied,
"Yeah, there they are," pointing to the top of Turtle Hill. "Doesn't bother
me, I'm used to it." After a pause he continued, "If they shoot at me,

that means they're not shooting at you all." I was moved by his warrior spirit, looking out for others.

I walked over to where my Zen friends were talking to another Native volunteer policeman. He was Christian, wore a Mohawk, and was a mixed martial arts fighter. He spoke softly and thoughtfully. Wendy suggested we pray together and invited him to lead the prayer. He declined but she was persistent. The four of us took one another's hands on what he had called The Bridge of Hope. "The one thing I pray for today," he said, "is for one of those police over there on the other side, just one, to come over here so we can have a dialogue. Just him and me. As people, not in our roles. A one-to-one dialogue."

Powerful moments in the spaces between what was organized.

As we were about to leave, the veteran policeman was looking through his binoculars and said, "They're mobilizing. They're preparing to move on the camp." A wave of fear, a traumatic ripple; our body-minds 'mobilized' too. We tried to figure out what they were doing and why. There had been no provocations. After a few minutes, he realized it was an hour past the time John Floberg had told the police the event would end. We were still on the bridge talking and so was a long trailer with packages of bottled water. After we cleared the bridge and the trailer drove off, the troops withdrew.

⟜≋⟋

A month later, on December 4, 2016, following a nine-month-long struggle and the arrival the previous day of thousands of U.S. war veterans, the Army Corps of Engineers denied the DAPL owners, Energy Transfer Partners, an easement to drill across the Missouri River. Joyful celebration ensued. Two months later, on February 9, on the orders of President Trump, the Army Corps aborted the Environmental Impact Statement in full progress and granted the easement. Drilling recommenced, and pipe was laid across the Missouri River, and the oil began being pumped, and leaking.

The burned-out semi-truck was removed but concrete barriers still kept the Bridge of Hope impassable. Police and DAPL security remained visible and continued to arrest water protectors praying on the hillsides of their ancestral lands. Surrounded on all sides by a mass of

National Park Rangers, Bureau of Indian Affairs officers, and highly militarized local and state police, residents either left, crossing the Missouri River and burning their teepees and structures behind them to prevent desecration, or were arrested.

A fiercely determined group of Natives and non-Native allies remained encamped nearby at the renamed Oceti Oyate, All Nations Camp, as they worked through record blizzards and sub-zero weather cleaning up the camp and preparing to move to higher ground nearby as spring arrived with warmer weather and the likely flooding of the plain.

The fire of Standing Rock continues to burn in protest camps in Pennsylvania, Louisiana, and around the U.S. and Canada. Recent revelations showed that a paramilitary unit, TigerSwan, modeled after Blackwater, had been providing security for Energy Transfer Partners. Their strategies were the same as those employed in the wars in Afghanistan and Iraq.

"The Intercept recently revealed how international private security firm TigerSwan targeted Dakota Access water protectors with military-style counterterrorism measures. TigerSwan began as a U.S. military and State Department contractor, hired by Energy Transfer Partners, the company behind the $3.8 billion Dakota Access pipeline. The investigation was based on leaked internal documents, which show how TigerSwan collaborated closely with law enforcement agencies to surveil and target the nonviolent indigenous-led movement. In the documents, TigerSwan also repeatedly calls the water protectors 'insurgents' and the movement 'an ideologically driven insurgency,' even using words like 'jihadi.'"

The Standing Rock Sioux Tribe won a major legal victory in federal court which may have the power to force the shutdown of the $3.8 billion Dakota Access pipeline. District Judge James Boasberg ruled that the Trump administration failed to conduct an adequate environmental review of the pipeline, after President Trump ordered the Army Corps to fast-track and greenlight its approval. The judge requested additional briefings on whether the pipeline should be shut off until the completion of a full review of a potential oil spill's impacts on fishing and hunting rights, as well as environmental justice.

The Standing Rock Sioux Tribe is preparing to build a solar farm in Cannon Ball, less than three miles from the Dakota Access pipeline, and aims to have all twelve communities at Standing Rock powered by renewable energy sources.

In July 2020, a District Court judge issued a ruling for the pipeline to be shut down and emptied of oil pending a new environmental review.

The temporary shutdown order was overturned by a U.S. Appeals Court on August 5, though the environmental review is expected to continue. Today, the pipeline remains open and continues its flow of Bakken crude oil following a Federal Court ruling on May 21, 2021 which blamed the US Army Corps of Engineers for inaction on a pipeline that will keep operating illegally for now.

FRUITS

Agents of compassion can easily become focused on the fruits of their actions. I recall as a resident at the Maui Zendo working on several projects, only to see many flounder. Change, systemic or personal, is both gradual and sudden, but mostly it is unpredictable and outside our locus of control. Euphemisms like "the best laid plans go awry," "no good deed goes unpunished," and Murphy's infamous law that everything that can go wrong will go wrong, all carry their own bit of truth. When we make common cause, we're working not with automatons but with people, and people have limitations. While serving as work leader, preparing food, or overseeing the dojo during sesshin, it took a while, with some feedback from others, to reign in my tendency to expect that things would go smoothly and harmoniously. We can engage fully, suspending the desire for perfection and riding herd on the tendency to over-correct. A truism but true nonetheless: we learn by example.

Today, our concern for our planetary climate emergency can make us chronically anxious and overwhelmed. Urgency and agency need to support each other. Yet, there are potholes – one is to become overwhelmed, helpless, and paralyzed. Another is hewing to achieving fixed goals, making us feel insufficient, or pushing ahead in ways that burn people out. Yet another is to forget that the rippling impacts of cause and effect are mysterious and unfathomable. We help and we give, and we want to see results. It's frustrating when we don't and we feel powerless. What gets us through is a hardy sense of agency, of feeling empowered, sincere practice, the company of sisters and brothers, and the ability to grieve.

A dear friend and colleague was nearing the end of her life, beloved friends were dying, the world was in shambles, and all her considerable efforts at helping make it a better place were, she felt, for naught. Although she had reached many people in her international efforts, this was depressing. She understood intersubjectivity in the consulting room and *liked the idea* I had suggested of concentric circles of beneficent influence spreading out like a mandala from each of the persons whose life she had touched. But this was not the way *it actually felt* to her. Could we say that she, like each of us, has an epistemological blind spot that coexists, metaphorically speaking, with an 'attention deficit?' Blake writes, and Buddhist intersubjectivity teaches, about seeing the universe in a grain of sand and eternity in an hour. Would such understanding, personalized, make her pain at seeing her time on earth end without achieving the 'external' standards of her dream easier to bear? Might she be more available to partake in and enjoy not only the 'smaller'-scale achievements but the ordinary moments that remain?

It's easy to ignore the joy of putting shoulder to shoulder in struggle, in resistance to an unjust existing order, say, in pioneering new forms and protecting ancient ones. The Buddha addressed our collective allergy to facing our and the world's pain by putting suffering as the first of his noble truths. But suffering is not enough. It takes a bit of non-suffering to transform anguish. Diligent practice helps us keep that light alive. It's not just dhyana, it's prajna. We may, as a species, destroy our world and the more-than-human world as well. Other species may replace us. But there is something that is not destroyed. Not something everlasting. It is not on the register of conceptual formulations such as appearing and disappearing, being born and dying. Classical Buddhists speak of "the deathless," but if it exists it is because the duo – birth and death – do not apply; they're absent. I'm not suggesting we become fatalistic nor that we think it's all going to be okay so not to worry; just go ahead with the business of extraction and destruction. To the contrary, I'm saying that while we work in the direction of turning things around, we don't have to cleave to a results-oriented agenda.

JOINING FORCES

This was the name of a program involving the White House and the Department of Defense established to bring together grassroots and governmental organizations to help vets. It never worked; it was just for show. Real joining was stifled because of territoriality and the refusal to share resources and truly collaborate.

The following vignette captures a bit of what I think real joining and coming alive together is. Jeremy Williams and his wife were struggling. After two long tours, he was drinking, shouting at the kids, and taking his exasperation out on his wife. The couple had broken up and gotten back together twice. They came to a retreat to improve their relationship and get help with Jeremy's post-traumatic stress and moral injury.

Retreat participants could elect to spend an afternoon kayaking on beautiful Tomales Bay. Jeremy and his wife won the impromptu family race back from Heart's Desire Beach. When they hit shore back in Marshall, Jeremy exclaimed, "Joe, I'm so high!" His and his wife's faces showed the natural high of being connected within themselves, between one another, among other veteran families, and with the sheer beauty of the great outdoors.

Aliveness is our birthright, but Jeremy had been unable to reclaim this quality after the adrenaline-fueled surges of the war zone. On the beautiful, rushing waters of Tomales Bay, together with his wife and children and other supportive military and veteran families and civilian volunteers, and our team of facilitators, he found a way once again to enjoy life-giving exhilaration and share nourishing connection. We knew we were on to something when, during the closing circles, participants' comments began to echo across retreats. They said they'd never experienced an environment this safe, this trusting, where they could be real and reconnect with their fellow vets, their families, and themselves – where they could risk letting their guards down, experience the belonging and camaraderie of service again, and open up as much or as little as they wanted. At the end of a retreat, as we were saying our goodbyes, one veteran said, "I'm not into organized religion, but this is how church should feel."

The healing sangha community is also a community of resistance; against war itself, against the corrupt institutions that fail to care for the wounded, against the military industrial complex and the war profiteers who thrive on war. We are also resisting with our wise and compassionate action arising with the alchemy of aligned dhyana, prajna, and sila. The Buddha gave a teaching about going against the grain. Now more than ever, we go against the grain by not allowing our conduct to be fueled by unbridled greed, hatred, and delusion.

It's not to say they don't arise. It's not to say we don't encounter them in ourselves, through tracking the traces of the impacts of our actions and plumbing the psychic fuels at play. But we understand how toxic the three poisons are. We don't cultivate them. We don't welcome them as roommates. They're just passing through. In this world of ours, it takes a certain fortitude to practice zazen and to have enough bandwidth and freedom to sit and follow our breath, work on our koan, or practice lovingkindness. That is itself an act of resistance in a world gone mad. We don't judge ourselves by external standards. I know many people nowadays are thinking, "What can I do?" I feel the same way. I want to be useful. I think we all want to be of use. But the world is vast and wide, and the web of interconnection, that connective tissue that links us all, the human and the more-than-human, is measureless. When we do sincere practice all beings grow.

All of us are different, and none is more or less important. Each part is essential for the whole, each expresses the whole distinctively, each part comes forward with its best and most unique idiomatic expression of their no-self nature, as the whole, and for the whole to exist. The conflict between self-realization and collective good evaporates. That is Buddha's dream. This is why it's so important to cultivate joy and, as Senzaki Sensei wrote, to "trust our own head."

Fueled by bodhicitta, the continuously purifying desire that all beings awaken (and its secular analogue, reparative intent), by the drive to represent our idiom, what we hold most dear – there is also an urge to participate, to be a unique part of something vaster, more connected, more inclusive than out own selves. More on this relationship between part, participation, and particularity in the next chapter.

5

STARDUST AND VITALITY

Thus shall you think of all this fleeting world:
A star at dawn, a bubble in a stream;
A flash of lightning in a summer cloud;
A flickering lamp, a phantom, and a dream.
– Diamond Sutra

My friend Allan lives on Starduster Drive. It's a great spot and I love the name. You and I aren't just dusted by stars, we are stardust, or so the scientists tell us. As awe-inspiring as this is, and as metaphorically evocative of the radical interbeing at the heart of our lives and deaths, it seems to posit an essential substance. In Buddhism there is no such essential-something.

How then can something that can't be measured, explained, catalogued, or pinpointed, that's not a "thing" at all, convey the Great Functioning (Yunmen), a fully functioning, maximally alive human being (Winnicott)?

There's a paradox at the heart of human experience. We must develop agency – a 'feeler' to feel, a 'thinker' to think, a 'dreamer' to dream – in short, a mind with which to bear and attend fruitfully to the states of mind we encounter and to learn from them. Yet, when this process is moving along 'well-enough,' there is no thinker, feeler, or dreamer – no mind at all apart from the living experience. A mind of one's own is critical, yet we only become aware of it when it doesn't work 'well-enough.' We might say that it is a background function that becomes concretized only when there's been a breakdown in good-enough 'othering.' This is reflected in the quote by the early psychoanalyst Ernest Jones: "I do not think that the mind really exists as an entity." Remarkable, and not that far from the Buddhist view that there is no fixed, permanent self-entity, but rather a moment-to-moment coming together and dissolving of states of experience.

Psychoanalyst Donald Winnicott (1949) writes of the tendency to localize the mind in the head or elsewhere and describes how discursive thinking can become an end in itself, a mind object, when the caregiver-infant mutuality is compromised and the infant needs to take over its own self-regulation and other mental functions prematurely to ensure survival,

> The mind does not exist as an entity in the individual's scheme of things provided the individual psyche-soma has come satisfactorily through the very early developmental stages; mind is then no more than a special case of the functioning of the psyche-soma. In the study of the developing individual, the mind will often be found to be developing a false entity and a false localization.[13]

Where is the Mind? The mind that "cannot be grasped" is, in Winnicott's words, not "localized" in time or space. The word *sesshin* (an intensive Zen meditation retreat) for example means to touch the mind, perceive and convey the mind. In Zen, mind is *empty*. Not vacuous but void of permanence. Rather, it's a field of potentiality. Our dualistic conceptions about reality form a discursive veil that obscures this living field. Although the mind has no 'thing' *in* it, remarkably it breathes, sits down, stands up, goes to sleep, shops, gets sick, laughs, and weeps.

When we look closely, we can't find a fixed entity, an ultimate agent. But it is just here – a sense of self, agency, and personhood operating silently, humming along nonconsciously, invisible, not impinging or obtruding – that we can let go of constricting, rigid and often trauma-derived identifications of self and of self and other. It is just here that the agency of compassion coalesces. Avalokitesvara, bodhisattva of compassion, at rest, sees the sounds of suffering and responds in accord, for the benefit of all. She knows it's not *about* her and she also understands it's up to her.

Ideally this true person of no rank has a full complement of capacities and qualities developed through conscious practice in and out of the dojo, and also by being aware that nonconscious elements such as psychic fuels, unconscious emotional experience and communication in the relational field are at play. So she understands the importance of tracking the traces of the impacts of her actions. She also retains access to idiosyncratic traits that have not been offloaded or dissociated, or if they were, have been reclaimed.

How does this happen from a developmental perspective? In Winnicott's framework, the child enters a phase where he doesn't spare the mother (parental figure) the full force of his aliveness. He "destroys the object," in fantasy and no longer protects the mother from his full-bodied energies. The object survives this destruction, and the child, internalizing this, is able to mix it up, make use of others and be made use of. He is able to contribute and participate, and can engage fully, drawing upon all the capacities and qualities, the traumas, the wounds and breakage, all of it.

We are most at peace, alive, and responsive when we are least self-conscious, self-obsessed, and self-preoccupied – when self as *klesha* is not operative. An *insubstantial person of substance* is one with robust capacities for standing and understanding, for not-knowing and for knowing. Formlessly forming, un-forming, and re-forming. Freely coming and going with a tutored spontaneity. Capable of holding life's joys and sorrows in the same hands. Making use of her idiom (Bollas' word for our distinctive aesthetic signature, our true self *activity*) in service to the liberation of all beings.

Stardust may not constitute our *final*, essential substance, but it is precious. We can break things down literally (or psychically) into finer and finer pieces until the chunks become dust and the dust becomes atoms and the atoms become particles – but we will never find 'it,' an essential substance. How is this so? Listen to my dear friend Dan Gerber's poem,

Often I Imagine the Earth
Often I imagine the earth
through the eyes of the atoms we're made of –
atoms, peculiar
atoms everywhere –
no me, no you, no opinions,
no beginning, no middle, no end,
soaring together like those
ancient Chinese birds
hatched miraculously with only one wing,
helping each other fly home.[14]

Helping each other fly home. In Zen lore, there's the archetypal figure of the ferryman, crossing beings over from Samsara to Nirvana. These two shores, like delusion and awakening, sorrow and joy, are not two (nor even one). It is the rowing, the crossing-over, the helping each other fly home that is the heart of it.

Dreams themselves are ineffable. Our life is a dream. Remember "Row, row row your boat." Our dreaming is not *Shakya*, but Buddha Joe, Buddha Larry, Buddha Carol. Personalized, able to stand, understand, and respond creatively; vigorously singular *and* interconnected, empowered, capable of agency, personhood, sense of self and ego capacities. Diligently continuing the work of *liberation on two tracks*, or, as Ken Wilber is saying these days, "Waking up and growing up." The presence or absence of these factors can determine our ability to live Buddha's dream vigorously. They are a major part of the continuing education of the Buddhist teacher.

In Zen, ghosts are amorphous creatures that cling to bushes and grasses. In terms of practice, when we are caught up in rigid, dualistic concepts, we're not fully engaged in our human lives. A true person of no rank is not defined by and does not stay caught up in such concepts as gain and loss, success and failure, enlightened and deluded.

But these bushes and grasses, these dualistic concepts can be sticky. They often contain dissociative residues that are reactions to overwhelming trauma and can become painful, obsessional loops. So, alongside diligent zazen, a true person of no rank may need to engage the Eightfold Path of Transforming Trauma, described earlier, engaging the process of turning ghosts into ancestors. These residues, as we saw, are unconsciously seeking the conditions and the setting in which to be safely represented, transformed and integrated. This, too, is part of the continuing education of the Buddhist teacher: meeting the traumatic shockwaves with ripples of loving discernment. Unhitching from narrow protective constructs of self and no-self means not being caught up in fixed, afflictive, identificatory habits. It doesn't mean being literally a nobody, trying to empty your head and psyche and behavior of what's considered 'self' as klesha.

A true person on no rank harvests her own
idiomatic uniqueness as she realizes and mobilizes
the kinship and diversity of all beings.

VITALITY

Aliveness, vitality, and the range of vitalizing emotions are important constructs in psychoanalysis. Recall Allan Schore's vibrant, almost musical account of the origin of these qualities:

> Secure attachment depends on the mother's psychobiological attunement, *not* with the infant's cognition of behavior, but rather with the infant's dynamic alterations of arousal, the energetic dimension of the child's affective state. [She] must resonate with the dynamic crescendos and decrescendos of the infant's bodily-based internal states. This activity occurs at an unconscious level. In these mutually synchronized social interactions, the psychobiologically attuned mother of the securely attached child not only minimizes the infant's negative states in comforting transactions but also *maximizes his or her positive affective states in interactive play*. Regulated and synchronized affective interactions with a familiar, predictable primary caregiver create not only a sense of safety but also *a positively charged curiosity, wonder, and surprise that fuels the burgeoning self's exploration* of novel socioemotional and physical environments. This ability is a marker of infant mental health.[15]

Vitality emotions are a bit like stardust in that they are not verbal and conceptual; they're automatic and embedded in a most intimate, though not necessarily conscious, register. In a paper on unconscious communication by psychoanalyst Tom Ogden, he writes that when meeting with a patient, he "listens for something human." Signs of life, aliveness. But this implies listening for something genuinely human. The manic defense (which erases emotional pain while fleeing into excitement) can *appear* to be aliveness; a thief might say he felt quite "alive" after a successful heist. However, it is through a discerning "resonance in truth" that something is perceived as truly human. Real aliveness is infused by truth. Climate deniers, anti-vaccine fanatics, white nationalist supremacists, militarist saber-rattlers, duplicitous heads of fossil fuel corporations, and others can get excited, be articulate and full of conviction. They can seem to be alive and full of vitality. But *in service to what?* What is the actual, not the professed, driving energy, the psychic fuel at play? And what are the outcomes? What do they leave in their wake? Tracking the traces, the impacts of their actions, will often reveal hidden intentions.

Change of Heart

Zen practice and the psychoanalytic process each offer an opportunity for an ethical 'turning' or change of heart, for both student and teacher, patient and therapist. Neville Symington once said to me that there is a difference between being selfish and self-centered. This became a kind of koan. Then, one day it dawned on me. Selfish, like elfish or reddish. Not just 'like' an elf or the color red, but expressing elfness and redness – *being* it. Expressive of self, *true self-ish*. One doesn't keep one's attributes all to oneself, but lives them expressively, thus giving them to others. One gives of oneself, 'gives it up.' A friend once inquired if Gandhi's aim in settling in the village and serving the villagers as best he could were purely humanitarian. Gandhi replied, "I am here to serve no one else but myself, to find my own self-realization through the service of these village folk." Self-centered or self-absorbed are indeed in stark contrast to this.

Truth is not something we attain or patch on. It's something we realize with a start, as if we'd always known it. Our self-protective delusions fall away. Turning toward truth, not just absolute truth but also the truth of our emotional lives can 'rock our world' and reveal hidden self-deception. While painful, it's also liberating and brings a certain joy, a joy that asks of us "not less than everything," as T.S. Eliot writes. It's the joy inherent in the attentiveness of the analyst and the Zen practitioner, the ongoing, engaged relinquishment and the empty but fertile ground charged with potential. In a paper on evocativeness, Applebaum writes,

> The heart of the ability to be evocative is heart. You have to be, not act to be. To care to engage one's feelings with those of another, to enter one's experiential world, to face the frightening warding off with determination and skill – all these are acts of love, and are experienced as such by the patient.[16]

Experienced as such. The psychic fuel operating is clear, the unconscious emotional communication received. Acts of compassion coarise with gestures of truth. The hard-won and continuously refreshed marriage of wisdom and compassion. One gives of oneself, something that can't be given, in creative abandon from the spacious ground of intrinsic affinity.

Embodying this capacity is perhaps the most profound and elusive freedom of all. It opens the door to "the dearest freshness of deep down things." The Zen teacher values insight expressed spontaneously; 'tutored' spontaneity implies an intrinsic ethics that incorporates the precepts.

THE POSSIBILITY OF GOODNESS

My friend and colleague Michael Eigen has never held back when describing the destructive elements in the human psyche. Imagine my surprise when I wrote him and received a message that concluded, "Lots of good…Mike." Lots of what? I wrote him back, thanked him, and wished him lots of good too. Not just good times, but goodness. Access to goodness, which has been an unnamed player running through this book.

I hear "goodness" and I think Goodie Two-Shoes. I have a horror of it; I was a "good boy" for way too long. The destruction-of-the-object-phase passed me by. I had to wait for early middle age to engage, to feel that "I belong to the world," and can and do have impact. "Trust your own heads," Senzaki wrote in his last words, "Do not put any false heads above your own." Don't go chasing Buddha and Buddhas out there!

Can we be five-tool players, doing the integrative work necessary for the marriage of wisdom and compassion in action (through dhyana, prajna, and sila) in the particulars of relational living? Can we trust our own goodness, the quality of our psychic fuels, our emotional maturity and spiritual ripeness? Trust and verify, tracking the impacts of our actions, realizing that liberation is on two tracks and engaging both in concert. The current invasion and brutalization of Ukraine drive home just what mad sadistic cruelty, what blood lust for power we are capable of. Greed, hatred and delusion do indeed rise endlessly. So let's not be naive. Like about our 'innate goodness.' Changing the lyrics, we do indeed "have the whole world in our hands." There but for the grace. If we are refining and purifying our intention – by attending bi-directionally to when and how it's *not* pure – then we can say let there be peace, and let it begin with me.

Spiritual practice and personal growth don't exist in a vacuum. They're not conceptual or theoretical. Buddhist realization and emotional maturity are both expressed in the particulars of daily living. Practice, study, and service go hand in hand. Insight and compassionate activity arise together and make one another possible. As we awaken, we discover our intrinsic kinship with the wider communities in which we co-exist: social, educational, political, and ecological among them. Zazen on the cushion and in the meditation hall, and emotional growth in the consulting room each finds living expression in the world. Inter-dependence-in-action is the fruit of mature spiritual practice and psychological growth alike: what benefits me most deeply benefits the other as well. When the other awakens and flourishes, I grow and thrive. We're in this together and we awaken in concert. While writing *Waking Up from War*, I had the unexpected pleasure of participating in an entirely ordinary scene that conveyed the experience of peace and benevolence.

I brought my broken computer to a fellow who lives in Hali'imaile, a small town that is home to some of the most majestic banyan trees in Hawai'i. While waiting for the repairs to be done, I sat at a picnic table under one such great tree, in a row of four massive banyans. As I waited, I began to relax, enjoying the serenity and beauty, letting go of my timetables. School had let out and two Hawaiian women were sitting on the grass 'talking story' while their children played nearby, checking in every so often to get a snack. An old man, short and thin, with gaunt cheeks, unevenly dyed hair, and a limp was slowly circling the area. He sat down at the table, kitty-corner from me. He didn't respond to my quiet "hello" and made no eye contact. We sat together quietly under the great tree for about twenty minutes. My hands were folded on the table.

No sooner did I take out my pad and pen than the man got up and walked away. He made his way to a spot in the sun where he sat down and folded his hands. A Zen phrase came to mind, "the formless field of benefaction." I wondered if, under the sheltering banyan with the families, me, the singing birds, and other living creatures, the man had been drawn to partake in a benevolent atmosphere. I thought how unadorned and uncontrived the goings-on were. I saw folks at our retreats just hanging out together during free time and understood how the same peace that permeated these simple events felt healing to veterans and their loved ones, not unlike the way I'd felt when I arrived at Plum Village in 1983. This relief, this rest; we realize we're *already* home.

There's nothing we have to do, nowhere to get, no one to become. There's no technique to apply and no worry about succeeding or failing. In this atmosphere, deep tangled strands of anguish loosen, obstructions fade into the background and lose their grip. There is ease and freedom. Here, under the great Hali'imaile banyans, Hawaiian women sit on freshly cut grass, rooted like the trees beside them. A husband returns from work, sits down next to his wife, stretches out and lays his head on her lap as his kids play with their neighborhood friends. They have all the time in the world.

I realized with a start: "Here it is, the 'X factor' – this is the activity of a safe unconditionally welcoming environment." We realize it only when we're *already* in the midst of it. Some retreat participants say, "We're not sure how we got there but here we are, feeling close, feeling good for a change." The elusive "there, there," so conspicuous in its absence in many caregiving institutions, is palpable. It's not a gimmick, it's just our beating hearts at rest, "immobilized without fear," as neuroscientist Steve Porges puts it.

This is how we realize and share the healing potential of our humanity. It is not an add-on, it comes built-in, would that we remember and seize the opportunity to connect with it. We can't manufacture or replicate it. It's unique each time, but the same, too. It can't be earned and it can't be forfeited. This bountiful source is always there. This feeling of connection, peace, and freedom is available in the particulars of our daily living. It is our true security. We are indeed home.

BEING A CHARACTER

"He's a character," people say. "A piece of work, a one of a kind, a work in progress." I'm drawn to some "characters," those who are themselves, spontaneous, and good. They've got their own flavor. There are others who seem self-obsessed and inflated. They have neither that flavorful kind of character nor the ethical kind.

Recall that Yamada Roshi said Zen was is perfection of character. Zazen, kensho and koan study are the vehicles. But in his old age, he realized these weren't sufficient. The basic spiritual qualities of kindness, compassion, equanimity, acceptance, and so on must be active. Character change is gnarly. It requires openness to a change of heart. It speaks to alignment, wholeness, integration, and along with these, the most elusive, integrity. Change happens beneath the threshold of awareness; it is imperceptible. Over time 'in service to what' becomes manifest: In service to all beings, this one included. A rich 'one pot' meal, simmering and simmering; a good sourdough culture.

In being a character, I also think of goodness, sincerity, whole-heartedness, humility: I haven't made all the possible mistakes yet; there are traumas yet to come up, and others still healing. Shakyamuni is still practicing and Freud is beginning his third or fourth analysis, this time not by himself. The best way to develop character, to purify one's intention, is to see – in action if possible – what is unwise, harmful. We almost always know this *après-coup*. In tracking the traces left by the impacts of our conduct, we don't just mean the relational impacts but opening to the self-deception that rides stealthlike beneath our conscious mind. Character requires not just opening to feedback from others about our impacts but it requires inwardly a kind of unconscious collaboration, an unself-conscious turning toward what arises, what is going on. This inner turning generates benevolent psychic fuels. Goodness has a chance when we risk becoming a character.

Let's turn briefly now to the original troublemaker we began this book with and whose poison words are its title, Linji. Aitken Roshi always urged us not to become complacent, especially when we had an opening, however modest. He would cite the spirit of the Linji line of Zen: "Not enough, not enough yet." Not enough what? Keep on practicing, and in our lineage deepen your eye, the eye of enlightenment, through continued koan study. I propose that it also refers to character development. I once had a T-shirt that I wore into the ground. On the back it said: "God isn't finished with me yet." Not enough alignment, not enough integration, not enough capacity for weathering the storms and responding wisely. Prajna is important but it is mired without being a character. Waking up and "growing up." The more we grow, heal as we need to, become fluent in unconscious emotional intelligence, and bring our hearts into accord with the intrinsic awakening of all beings, the bigger container we become to include all beings and actualize Buddha's dream. And the wider the repertoire of compassionate response accessible to us.

SAVING

Save the world? How did that get into the title. What hubris! Beings don't need saving; they're intrinsically enlightened, even if their delusions and hidden attachments prevent them from bearing witness. Nobody wants to be fixed, and when it comes to *homo sapiens*, there's no cure. Aitken Roshi would say we save them in our own mind, by including them. But what the world needs now is not only, as Dione Warwick sang, "love, sweet love." What the biosphere needs now is for us to save it from us, by treating the entire more-than-human world as partners in liberation. We need to save us from ourselves.

This book presents an expanded variation on an ancient story. It's a story about becoming fully human, for the benefit of all. It expands the narrative to include elements of our nature that are split off – emotions, traumas, and the unconscious. It's not a *better* story, but it may be a bit more accurate, parsimonious, inclusive, realistic and human. Can we, as Manjusri and Avalokitesvara, become renewable resources: insubstantial persons of substance and sustainability? I think this new story is in alignment with our natures, with how we operate, our behavior, conscious and unconscious – and our deepest intentions, conscious and unconscious. With an epistemology in which the common good does not oppose but co-arises with individual good. Is my liberation bound up with yours, or are you here to save me?

FROM PARTICLE, THROUGH PARTICIPATION, TO PARTICULARITY

We've seen how we are motivated by the reparative instinct, the desire to represent our idiom, and the thirst to understand our lives and deaths existentially. There's another important element: We want to *participate*, to be a part (and an expression) of something bigger than ourselves, to be of use. One of the thorniest binaries our world is grappling with is the zero-sum game: As my benefit increases, yours decreases. As your well-being increases, mine suffers. A variation on this is that when I'm part of a community or a collective my individual expression and well-being are compromised.

As threats to our planet and to the life it sustains intensify, and toxicity and violence spread like wildfires (and with wildfires), I've wondered why it's so difficult for people to realize that our own well-being and freedom co-arise with the well-being and freedom of other people, the Earth, and its creatures. Why is individual flourishing so disconnected from collective flourishing? The climate catastrophe and the ravages of the COVID-19 epidemic scream "we're in this together" – what's good for me fundamentally is good for you, our species, and the planet.

There are many in this era of intersecting cataclysms who are aware of this dilemma. On one hand, some exhort us to create unity: "We are all united, we are one," they say, usually adding that we are basically all the same. However, the worst violence in human history has spawned from desperate and brutal efforts to erase or cleanse difference and make us all one, all the same, pure. On the other hand, some think we are all irretrievably different and therefore should be physically separated one from the other. Oneness or proximity is the villain. At the extremes, the violent versions of both – we are all one, all united, or all different and separate – converge in the inability to integrate the other pole: the difference in oneness and the solidarity in difference. Out of an inability to forge an integrative understanding comes not just the absence of compassion but rampant blind violence.

The interpenetration of these two elements, 'the all in the one and the one in the all,' has been examined for millennia in various philosophical and religious traditions. In Zen, the verses known as the Five Ranks present a nuanced view of how the universal and the particular dimensions interact. Huayan Buddhism offers us the vivid metaphor of the Jeweled Net of Indra, and Thich Nhat Hanh used the felicitous word interbeing, to convey the way we literally compose and make each other possible. A piece of paper, he says, cannot be paper without the tree, sun, rain, and earth.

I asked socially-engaged Buddhist teachers about this on my podcast, *The Lotus in the Fire*. Some assumed I knew the answer and wondered why I asked. But I *didn't* know. And we didn't reach any answers. My friend, the philosopher, writer, and Zen teacher David Loy, expressed a similar perplexity, though from a different angle, when he asked, "Why is more always better when it can never be enough?"

In Zen practice, when we forget the self and unite with the matter at hand, we awaken to the vivid intersection of the particular and the universal. Our particular being is actually collective interbeing; simultaneously the collective cannot function without particular beings.

All beings by nature are Buddha, as ice by nature is water.
Apart from water there is no ice, apart from beings no Buddha.
– Hakuin[17]

But realizing this directly in Zen awakening or other experiences doesn't guarantee we will embody it, and if we don't live it, our species and countless others will go down the tubes. We're already over the edge. Can we turn things around?

Recently I watched a film about the life and work of physicist David

Bohm and was struck by how it shed light on these tough questions from a different integrative perspective. Bohm's innovations in physics, through which he sought an underlying, interwoven dimension to seemingly random and disconnected things, unfolded from his experiences growing up: a domineering and rejecting father and a mother with mental health problems that required periodic hospitalization. Bohm hoped that science would help people, and was particularly interested in ending poverty, but he came to believe that science alone could not do this. Like many of his colleagues he was interested in the 'Russian Experiment,' that is, Marxist theory taking shape in the USSR and its potential to improve human welfare: *From each according to his ability, to each according to his needs.*

Specifically, Bohm wanted to determine whether or not the collective imperiled individual freedom, as many in the West feared. His work would show, using experimental physics, that it did not: *Participation in the collective enhanced individual freedom.* This is a lesson for our times. Let's look at what quantum physics teaches us.

Quantum theory analyzes the world of fundamental particles at the micro level. Relativity theory addresses the macro level, the space-time continuum of everyday life. Bohm felt there was an underlying dimension in which macro and micro each found their place in an undivided wholeness. So did Einstein. In the classic double-slit experiment, scientists shot electrons through two slits, expecting that they would travel straight through as individual particles. They didn't. Once through the slits, the electrons dispersed into a wave-like interference pattern. This was inexplicable: A particle was a discrete entity and didn't express itself as a wave.

When experimenters attempted to confirm this puzzling occurrence, the electrons returned to behaving as isolated entities rather than waves. Is it a particle or a wave, an individual or the collective? It became clear that the lens through which one observes phenomena changes what one sees. Quantum physicist Niels Bohr said this paradox had no explanation and should simply be left to stand. Bohm and Einstein, however, thought there must be an undiscovered force or activity that could account for the seeming discrepancy, one that would embrace particle *and* wave in an inclusive register bigger than either.

In his *Hidden Variables* paper, Bohm hypothesized that electron movement was not random but rather was acted upon by waves that organized or piloted their movement. When his colleagues finally read this paper, they found it flawless, yet decided to ignore it. Years later, a team used computers to perform a simulation of Bohm's theory. Bohm was heartened when he saw waves on the screen organizing the electrons' movement. What he called an "undivided wholeness" accounts for both particularity and oneness, which he named the implicate and explicate orders, not unlike the particular and the universal, the phenomenal world and essential nature in Zen.

In the *Theory of Plasma Waves in Metals*, Bohm explored a new branch of science, plasma physics, and the behavior of electrons in plasma gases. Plasma is sometimes referred to as the fourth state of matter, distinct from solid, liquid, and gaseous states. This experiment produced results that piqued my interest and revealed parallels between the movement of electrons, individual human transformation, and the role of the collective. Bohm found that if you run plasma gas through the molecular lattice work of metals, something surprising happens: "To the extent to which an electron *participated* in the plasma gas," he wrote, "it became relatively free."

I think that Bohm and I, each of us in our own way, had the same question about the apparent incompatibility of individual and collective. It's counterintuitive: if I'm a member of a collective, it would seem conventionally true that I *don't* have freedom (a critique of applied Marxism and of Communist countries). But Bohm discovered that in the quantum world, to the extent to which an electron participated in the plasma "collective," it became free. What struck me about how plasma behaves was this possibility: to the extent that an individual (entity) – you or I – participates in the activity of the *whole*, engaging fully, to that extent it realizes itself and becomes, in Zen parlance, a true person of no rank, particular and distinctive, where all are "free to be you and me" (the name of a children's entertainment project).

Wallace Stevens expresses poetically what Bohm learned by pushing physics beyond its limits,

> Out of my mind the golden ointment rained,
> And my ears made the blowing hymns they heard.
> I was myself the compass of that sea:
>
> I was the world in which I walked, and what I saw
> Or heard or felt came not but from myself;
> And there I found myself more truly and more strange.[18]

PERCEIVING, DREAMING, AND CREATING

What are the implications of the scientific discovery that the lens through which we observe alters what we actually see? Let's revisit the impact of our perception itself: how we construe a certain situation by connecting the dots of sensory and affective data may determine how and what we experience. The brain is actively constructing models of reality moment-to-moment and readjusting these models based on updated data. It's not that we 'choose' or 'dial up' whatever reality we want, *carte blanche*. Rather, our assimilated, internalized, and personalized insights develop through ongoing attentional 'practice,' a kind of *dhyana*. They shape our very *perceptions*, and influence what realities – psychical and material – emerge for us, not only how we respond to them.

We see this in terms of expectations: Students who are expected (and perceived) to be capable of success are more likely to succeed. Experiencing a drug addict sprawled out on the street as a Buddha, a human being with dignity, rather than a bum will not only affect our response to that person but also affect and *create* that person. We could say that as we connect the dots of our sensory, visual, and other experience and bring forth a person (or other being) with dignity, we help liberate that 'other' from 'other' status so that he, she, or it can realize and share intrinsic awakening or liberation.

Our perceptions are infused and informed by a guiding myth, a dream, a philosophy of living. What are the understandings, motives, psychic fuels, energies, and spiritual qualities, that inform how we connect the dots? How we make links, derive meanings, act on these meanings, and perceive? Aitken Roshi would say that we live Buddha's dream. I say we live it out and create it moment-to-moment. It's the same with the psychotherapeutic dream of fully welcoming our disparate and disowned parts and experiences, as we widen the space of the heart. We are by nature in one another's dream; we are moment-to-moment dreaming one another. Nanao Sakaki has a poem:

> I sit down quietly in lotus position,
> Meditating, meditating for nothing.
> Suddenly a voice comes to me:
> To stay young
> To save the world
> Break the mirror.

We break the self-absorbed mirror and painful storyline we construct and sustain by participating in the vast and limitless belonging of our true nature. Currently many say, "It's just your story, let it go." But it *is* our story, our dream. It's what drives us, what we live and stand by, what actually gets communicated in our moment-to-moment interactions, no matter what our conscious intention. How we connect the dots – that makes all the difference in the world. This story is not ego-aggrandizement; it's what we live by, how we live, and what we leave in our wake.

And our planet? Since we are not fundamentally external observers but active participants in the web of interbeing, our conduct *is* the web itself, repairing, reweaving, revitalizing the biosphere. We are no longer an isolated particle. Forty-five years ago, a xeroxed, hand-stapled pamphlet circulated in Zen groups. The Vietnamese monk who wrote it began with a story about a couple who told him that caring for a new baby made it harder to find time to sit and practice. He asked them, "What if caring for your baby *was* your practice?" I liked that the baby's name was Joey, what I was called as a child. Our earth and all its beings are this baby, under our care. As active participants, coarising, we protect, repair, and revitalize it. As separable isolates – each man for himself, dog eat dog, grab it while you can – we destroy it.

Recall what Yamada Roshi said in his last words at the Maui Zendo in 1983 when he humorously but incisively presented a true person of no rank: "I don't know him at all! And we need him." I offer this poem...

Dust
I'm drawn to the trail this morning
called by a crispness
in the air, a quickening
in the blood

coffee on board I move out
on dry dusty trail turned
moist, dirt and rocks from the rains
give
to the step as soles, ankles
hips and knees slide
and glide for a change

bouncing through the coolness,
birdsong serenade brown hills
turned lush green,
angels abound

in La Ciudad de Los Angeles

Suddenly I'm stopped in my tracks,
"Whoa!"

through the trees, out across the valley
layered just behind the hills
in sharp relief – a layer of white
atop the San Gabriels

I turn my head from left to right, and back again,

only mountain tops, dusted with snow

A natural history of dust:

In T'ang China, the head monk presents his poem,

"The body is the tree of wisdom
the mind a bright mirror in its stand
at all times take care to keep it polished
never let the dust and grime collect"

A novice's goes next,

"Wisdom never had a tree
the bright mirror lacks a stand
there never was anything to begin with –
where could the dust and grime collect?"

Where?

Throw away tree, mirror, stand, dust, grime,
wisdom too!

A thousand mountains are covered in snow.
Why is this one peak not white?

This single peak, precious beyond price,

and what
a royal pain in the ass

No Buddha without beings

Without this peak, no

"Ah!" Snow dusting too

ABOUT THE AUTHOR

Joseph Bobrow is a Zen master, psychoanalyst and community activist. He has been practicing and teaching Zen for fifty years and is Roshi of Deep Streams Zen Institute in Los Angeles. Joseph has long been integrating Western psychology with Buddhist practice to create communities for transforming individual and collective anguish. Among these are a co-op school for young children, an educational support program for high conflict divorcing families, mentoring and meditation groups for incarcerated adolescents and young adults, and reintegration retreats that mobilize the power of community to help veterans, their families, and their caregivers transform the traumas of war and find peace.

Joseph tells the story of his integrative work and its applications to building peace in *Waking Up from War: A Better Way Home for Veterans and Nations*, with a foreword by the Dalai Lama. Joseph's first book was *Zen And Psychotherapy: Partners in Liberation*, with comments by Thich Nhat Hanh and foreword by Norman Fischer. *After Midnight: Poems of Love and War*, is Joseph's first collection of poems.

His podcast, "Lotus in the Fire," brings seasoned teachers and activists into dialogue on Engaged Buddhism. He practices psychotherapy and psychoanalysis in Los Angeles and teaches widely.

ENDNOTES

1   The Four Great Vows, *Diamond Sangha Sutra Book*, Diamond Sangha, 2020, Honolulu

2   *The Roaring Stream*, Nelson Foster and Jack Shoemakeer, editors, The Ecco Press, 1996, Hopewell, NJ, p. 174-5

3   Dogen, from *The Hazy Moon of Enlightenment*, Maezumi and Glassman, editors, Zen Center of Los Angeles, 1977, Los Angeles

4   *Master Yunmen*, edited by Urs App, Kodansha International, 1994, Tokyo

5   Ibid.

6   "Discovery of the 'Other'," Marion Milner [also known as Joanna Field], in *A life of one's own*, Tarcher/Putnam, 1981, New York, p.192

7   *The Palm at the End of the Mind*, Wallace Stevens, Vintage Books, 1990, New York, p. 54

8   *An Experience of Enlightenment*, Flora Courtois, Theosophical Publishing House, 1986, Wheaton, IL, p. 30-35

9   *Diamond Sangha Sutra Book*, Diamond Sangha, 1990, Honolulu, p. 1

10 *Zen and Psychotherapy*, Joseph Bobrow, Wisdom Publications, 2020, Somerville, p. *xxxiii*

11 Dogen, *The way of everyday life*, edited by Maezumi, 1978, Zen Center of Los Angeles, Los Angeles

12 *Call Me by My True Names*, Thich Nhat Hanh, Parallax Press, 1999, Ypsilanti, MI, p. 15

13 "Mind and its relation to the psyche-soma," Donald W. Winnicott, in *Collected Works: Through paediatrics to psycho-analysis*, International Universities Press, 1958, New York. (Original work published in 1949). pp. 244

14 *Particles: New and Selected Poems*, Dan Gerber, Copper Canyon Press, Port Toowsend, WA. p.177. The poem originally appeared in *Sailing through Cassiopeia* (Copper Canyon Press 2012).

15 From "The Neurotherapist," in *The Development of the Unconscious Mind*, Allan N. Schore. W.W. Norton & Company, 2018, p.11

16 *Speaking with the second voice: Evocativeness*, S. Applebaum, 1999, unpublished, unpaginated manuscript

17 "Song of Zazen", Hakuin Zenji, in *Diamond Sangha Sutra Book*, Diamond Sangha, 1990, Honolulu, p. 10

18 "Tea at the Palace of Hoon," in The Palm at the End of the Mind, Wallace Stevens, Vintage Books, 1990, New York, p. 54

ACKNOWLEDGMENTS

I want to thank Greg Harrison and John Briere for their keen, encouraging interest and numerous lively conversations on the themes in this book.

Our Deep Streams Sangha is a steady source of warmth, good questions, and stimulating comments. My longtime friend Susan Kerman read the proposal and provided useful feedback. The sweep of Michael Eigen's mind and his generosity of spirit have moved me.

My mother, Helen and my father Robert, were activists before I knew the word.

My old teacher, Robert Aitken Roshi, was ahead of his time in conveying the interplay of Zen practice and social action. I'm grateful to two other important teachers, Yamada Koun Roshi, and Thich Nhat Hanh. When Nhat Hanh saw a cloth copy of the Heart Sutra in my room at Plum Village in 1983, he said he hoped I would discover the real Heart Sutra.

To the many hundreds of veterans and their families, children, and caregivers I have had the honor of knowing, I am so fortunate to have shared the path of healing and awakening. To my patients, I learn more with you than you will ever know.

Joe Caston's moving poems and our enduring connection around our writing and lives are a rare pleasure. Thanks to Arnie Kotler for his editorial acumen, Larry Barber for proofing the manuscript, and my publisher, John Negru, of Sumeru Press for his faith in my work.

www.ingramcontent.com/pod-product-compliance
Lightning Source LLC
Chambersburg PA
CBHW021342090426
42742CB00008B/705